THE DEFENDERS

Happy Sailing

from Jerry & Tom

1972

THE DEFENDERS

Edwin P. Hoyt

South Brunswick and New York: A. S. Barnes and Company
London: Thomas Yoseloff Ltd

A. S. Barnes and Co., Inc.
Cranbury, New Jersey   08512

Thomas Yoseloff Ltd
108 New Bond Street
London W 1 Y OQX, England

SBN 498 06856 0

Printed in the United States of America

Contents

List of Illustrations

(Italic page numbers are facing pages.)

7

THE DEFENDERS

1

The Hundred Guinea Cup

In a glass case in the quiet of the New York Yacht Club's trophy room stands an ugly pot-bellied cup—the most valued prize in the world of yachting—called The America's Cup. The spelling of the name seems odd until one realizes that The Cup was named for the yacht that won a race against great odds and carried off the cup from England more than a century ago.

The America's Cup is nearly as old as yachting in America. The winning of The Cup and its uninterrupted possession by the United States since 1851 tell a proud story of American yachting. Although challenged by the best of England's yachtsmen, America has never lost possession of the famous Cup.

The races for The America's Cup began almost by accident. The Americans who first raced for The Cup in England in 1851 were not seeking a Victorian Cup, particularly one that would not even hold water. They had decided to take a yacht to England in trying to win a great deal of money. This was an age of business in America and these yachtsmen were businessmen.

In 1851 yachting was an old and honored sport in England. The idea of sailing boats for pleasure was imported from the low Countries in about 1600. During the following two and half centuries some Englishmen had become skilled yachtsmen, and since only the wealthy could afford to take the time to sail small pleasure boats, yachting was a sport for the very rich.

When America was settled some Englishmen brought yachts to the colonies. Some built yachts and small boats, and sailed them in and out of the coastal inlets and up the tidal rivers. But yachting really became important in America only in 1840, when the depression that followed the Revolutionary War ended.

In 1844 the New York Yacht Club was organized, and at about that same time other yacht clubs were formed in Boston, Charleston, and New

Orleans. In New York, Colonel John C. Stevens became the first Commodore of the yacht club. Stevens was a member of the famous Stevens family of New Jersey, which had long been interested in ships and railroads. A Stevens had been part of the Fulton-Livingston Monopoly, which tried to control all steamboat transportation in the United States in the early part of the nineteenth century. Another Stevens had competed with Commodore Vanderbilt, when the young captain Vanderbilt was running steamboats on the waters of the Raritan River and in New York Harbor in the 1820's.

So Colonel Stevens was a fitting man to be Commodore of the yacht club and sit at the head of the table in the little one-room shack on the Weehawken Flats on the New Jersey shore of the Hudson River. He headed a small, exclusive club. At first the members of the club owned only nine yachts. But nine yachts were enough for a race, and every autumn the members assembled to sail around a specified course. The race course ran from Upper New York Bay, through the Narrows that separate Staten Island from the Brooklyn shore, into the lower bay that runs along the New Jersey Coast, around a buoy at sea off Sandy Hook, and then back to the Upper Bay. Racing was made possible even with yachts of all different shapes, sizes, and rigs, by the adoption of a system of time allowances—small, slow crafts received a handicap, or a time allowance. If the yachtsmen aboard could navigate their yacht more efficiently than those aboard a larger, faster vessel, they could win the race even if the other boat crossed the finish line first.

Half a dozen years after the formation of the New York Yacht Club, its members decided to seek some sport in England. The occasion was coincidental with a great international trade fair in London, planned for 1851. Some yachtsmen in America decided that a native American schooner should be among the products exhibited there, for the Americans had mastered the art of building fast, maneuverable light craft.

In those days sailing ships had neither a wireless nor a telephone, so harbor piloting was an extremely competitive profession. The pilots maintained fast schooners which headed out to sea in the early mornings, looking for sailing vessels that wanted an escort into the harbor. Boats the pilots used had to be fit for any weather—they had to be able to stand out to sea, and they had to be shallow draft and sturdy. Speed, of course, was the very first requirement.

Some of these pilot schooners found their way into the hands of yachtsmen. They needed only small crews and their rigging was easily worked. So when the talk of racing in England excited the interest of Commodore Stevens, he joined with others in a syndicate to build the

America's **Cup trophy**

Model room of New York Yacht Club

Commodore John Cox Stevens

The schooner yacht *America*

America, a schooner modeled after the pilot boats.

The syndicate was composed of a number of wealthy men, including Edwin A. Stevens, the Commodore's brother, and George L. Schuyler. The model of the boat was built by designer George Steers who had built the famous pilot boat *Mary Taylor.* Steers followed the same sharp bow lines and slim hull that he had developed so successfully. Once the model was approved by the syndicate the yacht was built at the shipyard of William H. Brown, far up the East River at the foot of 12th Street.

The *America* was an expensive craft. Fully rigged, she cost $30,000, in a day when a dollar a day was good wage for a workman. She was 101 feet, 9 inches overall, with 90-foot waterline. She was 22 feet broad in the beam, and she drew 11 feet of water. Her mainmast was 81 feet long and her foremast was over 79 feet. Both were strongly raked (tilted backwards). The bowsprit was extremely long—32 feet from tip to heel—and the main boom was 53 feet long, swinging well out past the stern, She was gaff-rigged in the fashion of that period (*see* illustration).

Below, the *America* was built almost along the lines of a pilot schooner. Her sail locker stood under the cockpit, and her main saloon ran from the mainmast aft. Around the side of the saloon 6 berths were built. Forward were 4 staterooms, a galley, a pantry, and a forecastle which housed 15 berths. The yacht also contained a bathroom, a clothes locker and storage space, which ran along the passageways from the main saloon to the cockpit.

The yacht was delivered to the syndicate on June 11, 1851, and made ready to sail across the Atlantic and engage any comers in racing. When she left the United States there were some doubts about her abilities, for in her trials she had been beaten in a race with the centerboard sloop *Maria.* So, she was not the fastest thing afloat, however she was fast, maneuverable and a strong match for any yacht.

On June 21, the crew of the *America* stowed the racing sails below and unfurled the sea-going sails for the trip. The *America* was towed to Sandy Hook and there set out into the broad Atlantic. She carried a crew of thirteen for the voyage: George Steers, the designer; Dick Brown, the captain, a Sandy Hook pilot; Nelse Comstock, the mate; Steers' 15-year-old nephew Henry; and six sailors, a steward, and a cook. Colonel Stevens was not aboard, however he had made arrangements to travel by steamship and to meet the crew on the other side of the Atlantic, at Le Havre.

The voyage to Le Havre took twenty days, with one day's run logged at 284 miles. Three weeks were then spent refitting and preparing for races. The Earl of Wilton, commander of the Royal Yacht Squadron, had extended an invitation to the *America* to join the members of the Squadron at Cowes, on the Isle of Wight. Cowes was the headquarters of the Royal Yacht Squadron for the races that were to be held in a few days. Colonel Stevens and the crew, who were certain that the *America* could outrun any British yacht, hoped to earn more than the cost of the yacht in racing bets when the *America* sailed for Cowes on July 31.

Commodore Stevens arrived and anchored 6 miles outside the harbor, because when the *America* arrived dense fog shrouded the entrance to the harbor. A few hours later the English cutter *Laverock* came out from Cowes for a look at the American yacht. The *America* was weighing anchor and making ready to sail for the harbor when the English yacht came in sight. The Englishmen wanted to race.

Commander Stevens might have raced and "dogged it," but he did not. The wind was against them, so the two yachts raced back to Cowes. The *America* finished well ahead of the *Laverock*.

The English were impressed with the victory, but not favorably. English yachtsmen called the *America* a "racing machine," and a "big-boned skeleton." They spoke slightingly of the rake of her masts, her long bow and bowsprit. They said she ought to carry a fore-topmast, like almost all English yachts did, for they were sure the extra mast would give her more speed, and a proper look.

The English yachtsmen were friendly and hospitable to their guests, far more than most English noblemen were to most American businessmen. Other Americans came to visit England and were never invited to an English club, or to an English house, or to an English ball. Generally speaking, the English nobility looked down on Americans as people without breeding or culture. The treatment given the officers and crew of the *America* was unique for the times.

Good treatment did not satisfy Commodore Stevens—he had come to race and win money. Stevens tried to arrange races, but no one would race with him. He grew impatient at the delays and offered to race any schooner, regardless of size. No one answered the challenge. He offered to race any cutter, too. Nothing happened. The Commodore grew angry and posted a final notice on the bulletin board of the Squadron clubhouse. He would race any English vessel of any size, under any conditions, and for any sum of money, from one guinea to 10,000 guineas. (In other words, he offered to race for any sum from $5 to $50,000.) Commodore Stevens made only one stipulation: that they have a decent breeze—at least 6 knots.

No Englishmen seemed to be ready to chance any sum of money.

Finally, one member of the Royal Yacht Squadron, Robert Stephenson, offered to race his schooner, the *Titania,* against the *America* for a prize of 100 pounds. That was all. Even the British newspapers scoffed at the English yachtsmen, then. They compared them to pigeons who had been frightened by an American sparrow hawk. Commodore Stevens accepted the race for it was the only race he was offered.

Before the race with the *Titania,* the Commodore was invited to participate in the Squadron's annual open regatta around the Isle of Wight. All boats entered without any time allowance, although they ranged in size from the 47-ton cutter *Aurora* to the 392-ton, three-masted schooner *Brilliant.* The 170-ton *America* found herself right in the middle of the classes.

The London newspapers did not like the conditions the English yachtsmen offered the Americans for the race. "The course around the Isle of Wight is notoriously one of the most unfair to strangers that can be selected," said the *London Times* yachting editor. Neither speed of craft nor skill of seamanship counted nearly as much in such a race as knowledge of the local tides, winds, and currents.

Commander Stevens and the crew of the *America* were quite aware of this fact, but they had so much confidence in the superior speed of their yacht that they decided to race, even though there was not much to be gained by winning—only the 100 guinea cup put up by the Squadron.

On the morning of August 22, the day of the race, a light north wind was blowing in from the sea. The race was to start from an anchor position. The fleet was lined up, cutters in the front row and schooners anchored in a row 300 yards behind the cutters. The *America* was in that second row.

When the ready signal was made the crews of the boats would hoist sails, but the anchors would not be hoisted until 5 minutes later, when the boats would get under way as best they could. The signal was given at 9:55. *America* overran her anchor and slewed around. The crew lowered the sails and straightened her out, but by the time the *America* was under way, she was last. All the other yachts were well out in front of her.

It was a miserable start, but the *America* made up for it quickly. By the time she was 12 miles out, she had run through all the British yachts except four. One of these four was the litttle *Aurora,* the 47-ton cutter.

When the crews of the four English yachts saw the *America* overtaking them, they began to take action to slow her. The *America* was running wing-and-wing—her jib and foresail out one side and her mainsail out the other. The English boats steered close together so the *America* could not pass between them without fouling one of them. The *America* began cutting in and sheering off, to try to forge ahead, sometimes so abruptly that she was near a gybe—a dangerous maneuver in which the boom flashes suddenly from one side of the boat to the other, as the wind catches what had been the leeward surface of the sail. Had the *America* gybed she might have been dismasted and forced out of the race right there.

Twelve miles from the start of the race the yachts reached a point where they changed course to begin the next leg of the race. The wind was now off the bow and variable—the kind of wind under which the superior qualities of the *America* were best displayed. Tacking back and forth, the *America* left the four English yachts behind so rapidly, that when she reached St. Catherine's point there was not another yacht in sight. But there, beginning the third leg, the *America* caught the outgoing tide at its strongest, and against the tide she made little headway. (That was what the *Times* had meant about knowledge of local waters.)

After the *America* was slowed by the tide, the *Aurora* came up behind her, and the *Arrow* was third. Off St. Catherine's point, the *America's* flying jib was carried away. (Captain Dick Brown said he was glad it went, for he never did believe in carrying a flying jib to windward.)

That was the only incident. The tide slackened and the *America* came into a leading wind, carrying her at 13 knots toward sharp rocks called the Needles.

At 5:30 in the afternoon the *America* rounded the Needles. She was 8 miles ahead of *Aurora* and the rest of the Squadron was out of sight again. At the place called the Solent, the *America* found the tide against her again but this time it was worse—the wind dropped. *Aurora* came up quickly to gain on the American yacht. There is a story that Queen Victoria was watching the regatta from the Royal Yacht, near the finish line, and as the race neared its end an aide at the rail of the Royal Yacht announced that the *America* was leading, well out in front.

"And who is the second?" the Queen is supposed to have asked.

"Madam, there is no second," said her aide.

The incident probably did not occur, for the race was closer than that. At the finish, the *America* was 2 miles in front. She came in at 8:37. The *Aurora* came in at 8:55, and the *Bacchante* at 9:30. The huge *Brilliant* straggled in at 1:20 in the morning. A time allowance would have favored the smaller *Aurora*, but the *America* would have won anyhow, even if there had been a time allowance. (Using the Acker time allowance scale—which was in use in those days—the *America* would have won the race by 2 minutes. So the victory was complete.)

The English yachtsmen were annoyed by the victory of the American yacht, and called her many uncomplimentary names. They accused Commodore Stevens of creating a "shell" and said the whole yacht was a "Yankee trick." One Englishman said the British would do something about it.

"What will you do?" asked E. A. Stevens, brother of the Commodore.

"We will build a boat in 90 days that will beat the *America*."

The Englishman offered to wager 500 pounds that the Squadron could do just that, but the Americans scoffed.

"Twenty-five hundred would pay us for waiting 90 days," they said. "Make it 25,000 pounds and we will wait and sail the race."

But no English yachtsman would argue or compete with the *America* on that basis.

The next day, the crew of the English yacht *Brilliant* complained that the Americans had passed on the wrong side of the lightship at the Nab. The racing committee took up the complaint, but Commodore Stevens reminded them that he had not been instructed as to which side he ought to pass on. Since he did not know the local rules, he had no way of knowing something that the entire Squadron knew by by heart. The committee accepted his argument and the protest was not allowed.

But the aftermath of the race was not unpleasant. Some of the English yachtsmen were friendly. Queen Victoria went aboard the *America* for a visit on the day after the race. And a week later the *America* raced the *Titania* on a course twenty miles to windward and return, from the Nab lightship to the East to the Isle of Wight. The *America* won by 52 minutes, although she lost her fore gaff in the race and had to slow down to make repairs.

That race with the *Titania* was the last of the season for the *America*. Commodore Stevens and the syndicate had won 100 pounds and a shining silver cup worth a hundred guineas, and that was nearly all, although they had spent $30,000 on the yacht, and more on the fittings. There was one other item of profit: during the cup race they had won a flying jib-boom from Michael Ratsey, the sailmaker, on a bet.

Altogether it was a disappointing trip. The syndicate recouped a bit when they sold the *America* to Lord Jon de Blaquiere for $25,000, but their losses were still high.

Commodore Stevens came home that fall with the *America's* Cup, and placed it in a spot of honor in his house on Washington Square in New York City. The other five members of the syndicate agreed that he should keep the cup in his possession.

Six years later, however, the Commodore decided to give the cup to the New York Yacht Club, if the club would hold it as a permanent challenge cup, available to any organized yachting group in any country in the world that could win it in competition from the American defenders. So The America's Cup races were begun.

2

The First Challenge

In the next few years the famous *America* had many adventures. They began with her new owner, Lord John de Blaquiere, who thought he could improve the yacht's performance and her lines by shortening her two masts by 5 feet. His lordship either had some bad marine architectural advice or he was indulging a whim, for the *America* never performed as well with this reduced rig as she had with her own.

The following year, de Blaquiere took the *America* into the Mediterranean on a pleasure cruise, and encountered a storm so severe that he reported the sea was "all of a boil." The *America* rode the gale very well, thus answering the criticisms of her detractors that she was nothing but a racing shell. She was a yacht, and a very good one.

That summer, de Blaquiere raced his famous yacht for The Queen's Cup at Ryde in July, but the shortening of her rigging cut her speed severely. She was beaten by the *Arrow,* which had placed third in the great race the year before, and even by *Mosquito*, which had not placed at all. Later that year she raced privately against the *Sverige*, but the result was meaningless. *America* won, but really by default, because *Sverige's* gaff was damaged and she was forced to limp home.

The following year de Blaquiere sold the *America* to Lord Templeton, who renamed her the *Camilla* He used the yacht for only about a year, became tired of her and laid her up in the mud at Cowes where she sat and rotted for 4 years. Finally, She was was refloated, towed around to Pitcher's yard, the shipbuilding center at Northfleet, and completely and very carefully rebuilt of English oak. It was said that when the refitting was completed, she was sturdier than she had been in the beginning.

In 1860 the yacht was purchased by Henry Decie, who like many Englishmen in that time was a southern sympathizer. He raced her at Plymouth that summer, beating the English-built yachts *Wildfire* and *Galatea.* The next year he sailed her to Savannah on a mysterious mission, just at the time that the Confederacy was being organized and Major

Anderson was preparing his lines of defense at Fort Sumter. In April, as the Civil War began, the yacht was at sea again, this time, it was said, carrying several Confederate agents across the Atlantic, including Captain North, who was to take command of the privateer *Sumter,* then being built in England as a Confederate raider.

The *America* was raced almost immediately on her return, without any time for a refit or scraping of her bottom. She was entered in a regatta at Queenstown against three English yachts. She finished first, but on corrected times was defeated by the *La Traviata.*

That Summer the yacht was taken to Portsmouth and refitted for her last race in English waters against the schooner *Alarm,* which had participated in the famous race for the hundred-guinea cup, then as a cutter (a single-masted, gaff-rigged sailing boat). The *Alarm* won the race by 40 minutes, over a long course.

The novelty had now worn off the famous American racing yacht. Her detractors said she could easily be beaten. Her defenders said that was true only because her English owners had altered her design and outfitted her with loose, ballooning hemp sails, instead of the tight cotton sails laced to the boom with which she had won the famous cup. Yachtsmen soon tired of an argument that could not be settled, so in October, 1861, the yacht was sold to Gazaway B. Lamar, a southerner, and was sailed to Savannah where she was mounted with guns and used as a blockade runner during the Civil War, her name now changed to *Memphis.* She served for several months as a dispatch runner between various embattled southern points, and then one day she was chased up the St. John's River in Florida by a Union gunboat. There, in order to avoid being captured by the enemy she was scuttled.

Not long afterward the yacht was discovered by the Union ship *Ottawa* and was raised and put into commission against the Confederates, getting her old name back as she was commissioned into the Union Navy.

The *America* served for a time with the fleet that blockaded Charleston. There she was sent out after the fast schooner *David Crockett* which was trying to run the blockade. *America* stopped the Confederate ship after a brisk chase and brought her back to the fleet. She was also helpful, in the capture of three other Confederate ships, the *Royal Princess,* the *Georgiana,* and the *Antelope.* All of these, either owned by the South or under southern charter, tried to relieve the siege.

In 1864, the *America* was retired from active service as a warship and was sent to Annapolis for use as a training ship by midshipmen at the United States Naval Academy.

Three years before the beginning of the Civil War, Commodore Stevens

Sappho

Cambria

and the other members of the original *America* syndicate had given the famous cup they had won to the New York Yacht Club. Originally they said that the vessels simply had to be yachts of not less than 30 tons or more than 300 tons. The differences in sailing power of these various ships, of course, would be adjusted by the committee for handicap purposes.

The idea had created considerable excitement among yachtsmen for a very short time, but then the Civil War put an end to such pleasantry. It was not until 1868 that yachtsmen began again to think of international competitions, and that year the American schooner *Sappho* crossed the Atlantic to race against the English, as had the *America*. (Two years earlier three American schooners had sailed to England in a trans-Atlantic race which aroused some interest, but this was purely an American undertaking.) The owners of *Sappho* hoped to be able to do what Commodore Stevens and his syndicate had done in 1851—win several races and then sell their yacht in England.

A race was easily arranged. *Sappho* challenged two English cutters and two schooners on a course than ran around the Isle of Wight. She was very badly beaten, so badly that no English yachtsmen made an offer for her, and she was finally brought home.

That year, considering his easy victory over this American racing yacht, James Ashbury, who owned the winning yacht *Cambria,* wrote to the New York Yacht Club and suggested that he bring his yacht to America for a race. After much correspondence it was agreed that the race would be held.

Ashbury had suggested a far more elaborate plan for racing. He wanted the Americans to send a yacht about the size of his *Cambria* to England. The American yacht would take part in the English summer regattas. Then the American yacht and the *Cambria* would race back across the Atlantic ocean for another silver cup, and when they arrived they would race three times around Long Island, with the winner of two out of three races to win The America's Cup.

This plan was far too complicated for the Americans, but eventually Ashbury agreed to bring his yacht to the United States and race in New York Yacht Club waters.

The arrangements took time, and all the letters back and forth were duly reported in the press. Consequently, in the summer of 1870, when the *Cambria* was ready to make her crossing, people who were interested in yachting on both sides of the Atlantic had become quite excited about the race. The excitement was increased by an impromptu race arranged between *Cambria* and James Gordon Bennett, editor of the New York *Sun* and vice-commodore of the New York Yacht Club, who was cruising in

English waters on his schooner *Dauntless.* On the Fourth of July, 1870, the two yachts set out, headed for America.

The *Dauntless* was considered to be America's finest ocean-racing yacht. On board her that trip were Captain Bully Samuels, a famous racing skipper, Martin Lyons, a well-known pilot, and Captain Brown, who had sailed the *America* across the Atlantic when she came in 1851 to challenge the English.

The racing yachts were at sea for 22 days when a schooner's topsails were seen on the horizon off Long Island, and an excited group of yachtsmen waited to see who had won the ocean race. It was *Cambria*, they discovered, quite shocked. The name of the English challenger became very famous.

Newspaper writers in New York were very gloomy about the United States prospects of retaining The America's Cup after the *Cambria* defeated the New York Yacht Club's finest ocean-going racer. *Cambria* had come across the finish line just as *Dauntless* raised her topsails above the horizon off Sandy Hook. Only a handful of yachtsmen bothered to learn and understand that *Dauntless* had held the lead all the way but had lost the race by an hour and 17 minutes when the wind shifted in favor of the *Cambria* during the last 250 miles of the race.

After *Cambria* arrived in New York, bickering continued about the conditions under which she would race for The America's Cup. The difficulties were finally settled when the New York Yacht Club gave Ashbury the choice of racing against the club fleet over the club course, or not racing at all.

The race was set for August 8. The English challenger did not like the conditions, but actually they were almost exactly the conditions under which the *America* had raced in England, except that in the American race there were 23 American vessels pitted against one English vessel, with the sole object of defeating the Englishman so the cup would not be lost.

Among the defenders of the Cup was *America* herself, entered by the United States Naval Academy. No one expected her to win, of course, but there was much excitement in New York Harbor on the day that she was sailed in from Annapolis for the race.

All this while, the English challengers were complaining about the conditions of the race; however no one complained about racing such a yacht as the *America,* for she was a conventional deep-craft ocean sailing vessel. The English challengers did object to racing against the new American centerboard yachts, which had the great advantage of being able to adjust their draft, or the depth of water in which they could sail. (A light-draft boat, which can sail in shallow water, is almost always faster

Magic

than a keel yacht, except in very heavy winds.) Ashbury could not sail a centerboard yacht across the Atlantic and then compete, and he felt that the Americans should rule out their centerboard yachts, too. The majority of the yachts of the members of the New York Yacht Club, however, were centerboarded yachts, designed to sail in the shoal waters around Long Island sound. The centerboard yachts were sometimes known as "skimming-dishes," and were faster when running or sailing on a reach, although they did not sail very well to windward, compared to a keel boat.

On the morning of August 8, 1870, the fleet lined up at the beginning of the course. The start was off the Staten Island shore in the upper bay of New York, and the course was to run through the Narrows, east of the island, down the lower bay to the South West Spit Buoy, then to Sandy Hook lightship, and to return over the same course. The distance was about 38 nautical miles.

The wind that morning was blowing east of south, which meant that the sailing vessels would have to beat their way back and forth on the down leg to the Spit Buoy. Theoretically, at least, the wind favored the keel boats on the outward trip.

As an act of courtesy, the visiting *Cambria* was given the windward end of the line, with the old *America* next to her. Unfortunately just before the starting signal the wind shifted, and the *Cambria* found herself, instead of on the windward side of the fleet and thus in the most advantageous position, on the leeward side and in the most disadvantageous spot. She was not so badly off as *America* however, because the old sailing yacht was the last to get away from the start at anchor.

First to get away from the starting line was the little centerboard yacht *Magic*. She had her canvas up as the signal came and was quickly off, canting to starboard as she sailed toward the Long Island shore. The others, keel boats and centerboarders, were slower in starting.

Magic pulled out ahead, with a strong ebb-tide that helped draw her south. She tacked again about halfway between the marks of Owl's Head and Fort Lafayette and then stood in close to the shore, taking advantage of her shallow draft. On the port reach she was able to move out through the Narrows and took a lead that none of the other yachts could overcome.

America performed beautifully. Starting last, she walked through the fleet, passing the boats one by one until she was in second place and only 4 minutes and 55 seconds behind *Magic* when they reached the Spit Buoy.

Cambria had fallen far behind by this time. She was in twelfth place when the yachts rounded the Spit Buoy and began the sail for the next position at Sandy Hook. *Idler* and *Dauntless* passed *America* on this leg, so she was fourth as they rounded the lightship, which marked the halfway point of the race. *Cambria* had come up to eighth.

The sail back to the Spit Buoy was a broad reach, which meant the yachts could put on every inch of canvas they owned, and they did. At the lightship hundreds of small vessels stood just out of the line of the boats, carrying an estimated 20,000 watchers. That was some indication of the interest that had been aroused in this race.

As the racers rounded the lightship they stood as follows (estimated by the timers):

	hours	minutes	seconds
1. *Magic*	2	05	16
2. *Idler*	2	08	40
3. *Dauntless*	2	09	48
4. *America*	2	15	25
5. *Silvie*	2	17	23
6. *Phantom*	2	19	59
7. *Madgie*	2	21	14
8. *Cambria*	2	27	19

Of these yachts, five were centerboard vessels: *Magic, Idler, Silvie, Phantom,* and *Madgie.* Three were keelboats: *Dauntless, America,* and *Cambria.*

Magic flew on ahead, never really challenged. *Cambria* moved up, although some said she had no chance of catching the leaders. The debate was ended, however, when *Cambria* rounded Sandy Hook. Her crew decided to make up time by gybing around the Spit Buoy for the run to the finish. The gybe is a tricky and dangerous nautical maneuver at any time, because it involves allowing the wind to come around behind the canvas (instead of taking the boat around facing through the wind). There is a moment, when the full force of the breeze slaps into the sail, when the pressures are at their greatest, straining every strength of the masts and sails and canvas. Many a good sailor has lost his masts or has watched helplessly as his stays parted and canvas split when trying a gybe.

Cambria was making ready for the last desperate run, and getting ready to gybe, when a puff from the land, so strong that the sailors called it a squall, struck her and carried away her fore-topmast.

The loss of sail and the tangle of rigging—even for a few minutes—was enough to pull her back. Although she made the gybe safely around the buoy, she could not gain on the leaders because she could no longer spread all her canvas. *Cambria* finished eighth, as far as crossing the line was concerned, but when the officials corrected the times by allocating the handicaps to the various boats, *Cambria* was thrown back into tenth place.

Probably there was no chance for *Cambria* at best. She drew 12 feet of water, as opposed to the average of 5 feet by the American centerboard vessels. The first three yachts in the race were all centerboards: *Magic, Idler* and *Silvie,* and several of the keel boats finished after *Cambria.*

After the defeat, Ashbury kept *Cambria* in American waters for the remainder of the season and accompanied the New York Yacht Club on its annual cruise. There were a number of races on the Newport course, but *Cambria* came out second in all of them except one race with *Idler* in which that yacht parted a stay and had to go about until the damage was repaired.

At the end of the season the English boat was sailed home, but she was not to race again. She was sold to new owners who took her to West Africa in the coastal sailing trade, and there she worked as a commerical vessel until one day she was lost at sea in a sudden storm.

Ashbury was not ready to give up after the *Cambria's* sale. In fact several yachtsmen on both sides of the Atlantic said they thought the *Cambria's* design was superior, but that she had been hampered by a clumsy rigging. Ashbury agreed, but he also wanted a new design. So when he returned to England and disposed of *Cambria,* he commissioned the famous Ratsey's shipyard at Cowes to build another racing yacht. He wanted one, he told the shipbuilders, which would bring home the hundred-guinea cup to stay.

3

Mr. Ashbury's Second Try

The designers at Ratsey's yard in Cowes claimed that the new schooner they were building for James Ashbury, the *Livonia,* was the finest sailing ship of its kind in the world. She weighed 264 tons, drew 12 feet, 6 inches of water, and her mainmast from tip to deck was 68 feet long. Her foremast was only 4 feet shorter, and for her day she was regarded as a tall-masted sailing ship. An American sailing captain who heard of her was amazed at that length of masts: they were 13 feet longer than the masts usually placed in warships of 2000 tons, he said.

While the *Livonia* was being built, James Ashbury engaged in correspondence with the New York Yacht Club. He said he thought it was unfair of the club to demand that he sail against the entire club fleet. He believed he ought to be able to race against a single yacht chosen by the New York Yacht Club, and that the winner of the race or races ought then to be declared winner of the old hundred-guinea cup.

The governors of the New York Yacht Club would not accept this view, but Ashbury had another idea. He said he would accept the yacht club's position, however he would also arrange for a number of English yacht clubs to issue challenges for The Cup, and each challenge would name the *Livonia* as challenger. He would then have the right to race as many times for the cup as there were challenges—perhaps 10 or 20 times. The New York Yacht Club governors saw that this could become ridiculous. They approached George Schuyler, the last living member of the original *America* syndicate, and he was not very kind when he commented on the stiff position taken by the club's board of governors.

"It seems to me," he said, "that the present ruling of club renders the *America's* trophy useless as a Challenge Cup: and that for all sporting purposes it might as well be laid aside as a family plate. I cannot conceive of any yachtsman giving 6 months notice that he will cross the ocean for the sole purpose of entering into an almost hopeless contest for The Cup . . ."

He suggested that the yacht club accept the usual definition of "match" to govern the running of the race. "After all," he said, "in horse-racing,

26

Livonia

George L. Schuyler

when two horses were pitted against one another, it was a match. When another horse was entered, it became a sweepstakes."

The rulers of the New York Yacht Club, having asked for the advice of the last member of the original *America's* group, were placed in a very difficult position. They did not want to take that advice, and it was only after a great deal of grumbling that they accepted the more sportsmanlike way. Even then, they insisted on reserving the right to pick any yacht they chose to race against the challenger and proposed to choose four of their fleet as potential defenders, picking the one that would actually race only on the morning of the contest. This meant that the yacht club could pick four entirely different types of sailing yachts, and then, on the day of the race, pick their defender according to the weather.

There were two other points at issue. First, Ashbury did not want to race his keelboat against a centerboarder. Second, he said the course ought to be laid outside Sandy Hook and the tricky waters of New York Harbor, because the navigation of those waters took considerable practice and the victory might not depend nearly so much on yacht or sailing ability as on knowledge of the local waters. This second objection was reasonable enough, although the committee remembered how the British yachtsmen had taken advantage of local knowledge in the original race for the hundred-guinea cup.

On the first issue the New York Yacht Club would not compromise, and Ashbury gave in with good grace. On the second issue there was a compromise. This new challenge would be met in seven races. The course would alternate between the inside course which was the regular yacht club race course, and the outside course, which would be run twenty miles to windward and return from the Sandy Hook Lightship. This latter compromise was most reasonable. The committee could be counted on to choose the inside course for the first race, thus making sure that it would also be the last course if the meet went to seven races. But three of those races would be out in the open sea, and by the seventh race, if it went so far, the Englishmen could be expected to learn any secrets of the inner course.

Ashbury then did something the Americans did not like; having won his point about sending a single yacht to race a single yacht, he still sent twelve challenges from twelve British Yacht Clubs, each naming the *Livonia* as challenger, and he insisted that it was his right to enforce the twelve challenges. If he won any one of the races, then the cup would return to Britain.

James Gordon Bennett, Jr., Commodore of the New York Yacht Club, received this astounding demand. Ashbury was commodore of the Royal

Harwich Yacht Club and a member of all the other eleven clubs. The demand was refused, but eventually a compromise was reached, which involved the seven races instead of one.

The negotiations were extended and sometimes sharp in tone on both sides, but they were concluded in good will, with the American club agreeing to waive the 6 months notice clause so there could be a race in the fall of 1871.

The *Livonia* sailed from Cowes on September 2 and encountered very bad weather, including a hurricane which forced her to heave to and ride out the storm. She lost sails, broke her foreboom and lost her bowsprit to the angry sea and wind. After 29 days she finally arrived off Staten Island.

The New York Yacht Club chose its fleet of four defenders. The centerboard schooner *Columbia* and *Palmer* were selected. So were the keelboats *Dauntless* and *Sappho*. The first two were noted for their speed in light winds. The keel yachts were known to be extremely sturdy and fast in heavy weather, and the *Sappho,* which had not done at all well in challenge races she had sailed in England three years, earlier had been re-rigged and considered to be a very fast boat.

The first race was scheduled for the morning of October 16. Thousands of New Yorkers made their way down to the harbor to watch from shore and to board any small craft they could. Scores of small boats and yachts had come in from every club and haven along the east coast, and they clustered around the starting line where the yachts lay at anchor. Taking the advantage of naming a boat to suit the weather, the New York Yacht club committee chose *Columbia* for this first race, because the wind was from the northwest and only light to moderate.

At the starting gun, both boats slipped their mooring cables, sheeted home their headsails, and began moving in the breeze— *Columbia* heeling more and making better headway than the heavier, deeper, challenger. Within a mile and a half the lighter vessel had taken a commanding lead of 3 minutes. By the outer mark at the lightship she was 14 minutes and 38 seconds ahead—the spectators were yawning. Only a disaster could make a contest of the race, and at one point it seemed that the disaster might have struck. *Columbia* had gone a full 40 minutes ahead, when she came under the Staten Island bluffs and was becalmed. *Livonia* began to close up, but the gap was too great. *Columbia* inched her way through the intermittent light breezes but still came home 25 minutes and 28 seconds ahead of the British challenger.

Seeing the breeze that morning and knowing that they would be racing one of the centerboard yachts with their shallow drafts, the British challengers had known they had small chance of winning. They placed

Columbia

more hope, however, in their chance in the second race which was to be sailed two days later. This was to be the first deep water race of the series, sailed outside the harbor, and the challengers expected heavier winds to help them.

The course was laid out to the disadvantage of a yacht that worked well in sailing into the wind, because it called for a reach out and a reach back. Something was amiss in the course-making that day: *after* the morning had come and the weather was observable, the course was altered, laid east-northeast, or fully four points off a true leeward and windward course.

The committee debated long and hard, and eventually chose *Columbia* to sail again. She was, like most centerboard yachts, good in the light winds that were blowing, and good on reaching, or before the wind.

Like all centerboarders she was not so strong at windward work, and some said that this was perhaps why there was to be no windward work that day.

There was another strange incident before the starting. When sailing instructions were issued, nothing was said about the way that the boats were to turn the outer mark of the course before heading home. The captain of *Columbia* noted this and went aboard the committee boat for further instructions. He was told that it could be left on either hand, that is, turned from either side. Nothing about this was said to the crew of the *Livonia*. The sailing rule in England was that when no instructions were given, all marks were to be left to starboard.

The breeze picked up before the race began, and the Americans who had chosen *Columbia* instead of *Dauntless* for this day suddenly were doubtful of their choice.

When the starting gun was fired, *Livonia* came across the line first and set all her sails. She reached the stake-boat which had been moored at the far end of the course, a full 2 minutes ahead of the *Columbia*, but in order to keep the marker on her starboard quarter, she had to bear away and gybe around. This forced her to move out to leeward, cut her speed, and wasted time until she could pull her sheets in tight for the close reach home to port.

The *Columbia*, having instructions not given the *Livonia*, had a much easier task of sailing. She came up to the buoy, turned into the wind, keeping the buoy on her port quarter, and luffed, or let the sails go slack as she turned. Then, around the buoy neatly, the wind came at her from the opposite side, and she lost no time at all in setting a straight course for the long reach home. She cut in to windward and was soon in the lead.

Neither boat made a single tack on the way home. The wind hardened to become a moderate gale, and the lighter *Columbia* was forced to take in sail, because her rigging could not stand the pressure. She brought in her topsails and furled the foresail.

Livonia, faster in this kind of weather than *Columbia,* and built for just this sailing, carried all her canvas all the way home. She still could not catch the *Columbia,* which crossed the line 5 minutes and 16 seconds ahead. Further, *Columbia* was given a time allowance of almost exactly the same amount, because of her smaller size, and the official result came out that *Columbia* had won by 10 minutes, 33 3/4 seconds.

The English challengers were truly annoyed when they saw *Columbia* turning into the wind around the buoy rather than taking the gybe that would have put her out of position, too.

As soon as the *Livonia* crossed the finish line, Captain Ashbury made a protest. He said *Columbia* had violated the sailing regulations. He also said that the course was to be windward and return and at no time was it to windward.

There was no question in anyone's mind that had there been a 20 mile beat to windward on the return, the *Livonia* would have defeated the *Columbia.* There was no question that if *Columbia* had not turned around the buoy into the wind instead of gybing as did *Livonia* that the race would have been very close indeed, even given *Columbia's* time handicap.

Captain Roland Coffin, who sailed in the crew of the *Columbia* that day, saw how badly the differences in interpretation and misunderstandings had affected the *Livonia,* however the committee did not. In fact Ashbury did not ask that the victory be awarded him; he merely asked that it be declared no race and that the race be run over. The committee did not accept the protest.

The third race was a fiasco. The *Columbia* was chosen again on the morning of the race, because the *Dauntless,* which was supposed to make it, had trouble with her rigging. The crew of *Columbia,* having participated in two races and assured that they were to have a day off, had spend much of the night celebrating, and were in no condition to race at all, nor had they paid the necessary attention to their yacht.

It was after noon before the race began. *Livonia* was first over the line, and soon was in the lead, running the inside course. She led as they approached the Spit Buoy, but *Columbia* was coming up. Then, rounding the buoy, the fore-topmost stay of *Columbia* gave way, and the jib-topsail broke loose and streamed to leeward like a flag in the wind. The *Columbia* took 6 minutes clearing the sail, and at the lightship she was a mile astern of *Livonia.* On the way home she broke her steering gear and became unmanageable and truly out of the race. Her mainsail had to be run down, and she came up the bay under fore canvas, limping all the while. She was, in fact, 19 minutes and 33 seconds behind *Livonia,* although her time allowance cut about 4½ minutes off this figure.

By the American count it was now two races for the Americans to one for the English. By the English count it was one race apiece, with a disputed race hanging between them. Later, when the New York Yacht Club officials refused to resail the disputed second race, Ashbury claimed it his on the protest, but this claim was ignored.

The fourth race was held over the outside course, between *Livonia* and the keel yacht *Sappho,* which Commodore Ashbury had defeated so handily with his *Cambria* in English waters in 1868.

Sappho, by all accounts, beat the *Livonia* across the starting line simply by exercise of superior seamanship. Then the boats sailed in position as they beat out to the stakeboat, until the wind freshened or strengthened, and the *Sappho* began to show that her new rigging had made her a very fast boat. With topsails aloft, she put her lee rail under water, and sped along, passing *Livonia* neatly, and drawing 2 miles or 28 minutes ahead at the outer mark. On the home run she increased her lead, and when the race ended she was 31 minutes, 14 seconds ahead, plus an allowance of 2 minutes, 7 seconds which she certainly didn't need that day.

So the score was three for the Americans and one for the English, as the fifth race came up. The Americans took the position that if they won this race the series was over, for they would have taken four of seven. But Commodore Ashbury did not see it that way at all. He had sailed the second race and protested, and he sailed all the other races declaring that he was not giving up his protest. He even offered to take the matter to court for decision, a declaration that made few friends among the hosts at the New York Yacht Club.

The fifth race was again between *Sappho* and *Livonia.* At the start the English yacht was in the lead, but on the outer run to the lightship she was passed by the *Sappho,* and on the beat back against the wind to the Spit Buoy *Sappho* moved well ahead and was in position to take every advantage of the wind for the run home before it on the last leg. She won by more than 25 minutes.

As far as the Americans were concerned it was all over. Commodore Ashbury, however, said that he would now either sail the next two races or contest them and claim them if the United States boats would not race with him.

"The *Livonia* will be at her station tomorrow for Race No. 6," he wrote, "if the committee decides to entertain my claim. If not, I hereby give you notice that I shall sail 20 miles to windward and back, or to leeward, as the case may be, and as already requested I notify you to send a member of the club on board to see that the rules of the club are complied with. If no competing yacht is at the station, the *Livonia* will sail over the course, and also on Wednesday, the 25th, at the same time."

On the next day, the New York Yacht Club did not even answer his letter, so Commodore Ashbury arranged a private race with the *Dauntless* and the two yachts sailed the 20 miles-to-windward and return. *Dauntless* won, and Commodore Ashbury was beaten again, but so angry was he that he chose to state that he had sailed the course and the yacht club had not put forth a defender. Then, after the next day when the yacht club did not defend, he claimed The America's Cup by default.

The Commodore's claims and the acerbity of the New York Yacht Club, plus all the confusions and petty decisions that had been made on both sides reflected very unfavorably in both countries, and brought about a considerable amount of ill-feeling in yachting circles on both sides of the Atlantic. Ashbury accused the New York Yacht Club of unsporting conduct and he threatened that if ever he came to the United States again to challenge for The Cup he would bring his lawyer and take the matter to the courts.

The officials of the New York Yacht Club were equally bad-tempered. They returned three cups that Commodore Ashbury had presented to the club in good faith in the previous year when he had challenged with *Cambria*. The officials also spoke harshly of the sportsmanship of the Commodore in bringing his twelve challenges and in his conduct while in America.

Altogether the second challenge round was as poor a display of international sportsmanship on both sides as had ever been seen between the two countries in time of peace.

4

The *Madeleine* Defends

When James Ashbury returned to England and began visiting his twelve yacht clubs, he traveled from the Thames to Ireland, talking about the rudeness and unsportsmanlike conduct of the Americans of the New York Yacht Club to such men as the Duke of Edinburgh and the Earl Londesborough, and several knights and squires, all of whom were his fellow commodores of the clubs. Within no time at all the Americans had received such a black name that the gentle yachtsmen of the British Isles decided to foreswear further competition for The America's Cup.

The rules were obviously unfair to the challenger, and soon all the world knew it. In New York there was a party within the New York Yacht Club which spoke loudly of keeping the same conditions under which the United States representative had won The Cup, and in the embittered discussions in the press of both nations this view was aired loudly and often.

The governors of the New York Yacht Club were plain-spoken in the defense of the committee's actions, and the "preposterous" claims of Commodore Ashbury were subject of much sneering in New York club rooms. Yet one year went by, and two years and three years, and four, and no British challengers arose. It became apparent then, that there was very serious feeling among yachtsmen across the Atlantic against attempting to win The Cup under conditions the British yachtsmen considered to be totally unfair. Some members of the yacht club began to believe that there would never again be a challenge, as some British yachtsmen so spitefully suggested.

Then, one day in 1876, a letter came from the Royal Canadian Yacht Club of Toronto offering a challenge for The Cup. The governors of the New York Yacht Club were so pleased that they accepted the plea that the 6 months notice clause be waived so the races could be held that year, and further, some generous spirits in the club offered three races, to be sailed alternatively over the inner and outer courses off New York City,

33

with the final race to be decided by lot, or even to move to the open sea off Newport, Rhode Island, at the end of the Yacht Club's annual cruise.

The Canadians asked for more. They proposed that the New York Yacht Club select a single defender to meet the challenge, rather than selecting a field of defenders from which the best boat for the weather conditions could be chosen on the day of the race. This request was the subject of considerable newspaper comment and much discussion within the club, before the committee met to decide by vote. Eleven members voted for liberalizing the terms of the challenges and five members voted to keep the conditions as they had been. So the Canadians were to have an absolutely fair chance to win The Cup if they could produce a superior yacht and sail it better than the Americans could sail their defender.

Major Charles Gifford, the vice-commodore of the Royal Canadian Yacht Club, had issued the challenge in behalf of a yacht being built by a syndicate. The designer of this yacht was a Canadian boat builder named Alexander Cuthbert who had built several fast yachts that sailed on Lake Ontario. One of these had challenged and defeated an American-designed yacht which was supposed to be the fastest craft on the lake, and this had led to the forming of the syndicate and the plan for racing for The America's Cup.

The Canadian challenger was to be called *The Countess of Dufferin.* She would be 107 feet long, overall, with a beam of 24 feet. She was a centerboard boat, like most of the American yachts, and she drew only 6 feet, 6 inches of water.

Having made the challenge, the syndicate of the Canadian club then ran short of funds while *The Countess of Dufferin* was being built. There was some talk of financing the end of the construction and the challenge by public subscription, but nothing came of it. What did happen was that the challenger was finished as cheaply as possible, with rough planking, and rough, poorly designed rigging (which was most harmful to her speed and performance). Her sails did not fit her properly, and her bottom was not smoothly finished—both matters that affected her speed.

The Canadian schooner arrived in New York on July 18, 1876, after sailing down the St. Lawrence River and around the coast of Maine, then down past Cape Cod and through Long Island sound. She was hauled out of the water so that as much as possible could be done to smooth her rough outer planking. Her sails were sent out to an American sailmaker to see if they could not be made to fit the yacht better. They were recut in the American shop, but they did not fit much better afterward than they had fit before.

To try her out, Major Gifford entered the Brenton Reef Race, which

Madeleine

The Countess of Dufferin

was sailed over an ocean course. *The Countess of Dufferin* could not compete officially since she was a foreign yacht, but she could try her speed against the Americans in this race, and she did. Five yachts set out over the course of 275 miles. Last to finish was the Canadian yacht, for her rigging gave trouble all the way.

Major Gifford was distressed by the poor performance of the yacht, and asked some postponement of the races while the syndicate put the challenger into drydock again and had new sails made.

The Americans agreed. They named their own challenger at about this time. She was to be the *Madeleine,* a centerboard schooner which had been first designed as a sloop when she was built in 1868. She was about the same size as *The Countess of Dufferin*—107 feet long with a beam of 24 feet. She had won more races than any other American yacht in the last few years and was regarded as the best American sailing craft afloat.

The first race was finally set for August 11, and *The Countess of Dufferin* was towed down from Greenwich where she had been berthed for her refit. She made a sharp contrast to John S. Dickerson's *Madeleine.* No expense had been spared to get the American yacht ready for the race. Her bottom was newly coppered and smooth as glass. Her deck planking had been rubbed down until it shone in the sun. *The Countess of Dufferin* was still a rough specimen.

The course was to be the New York Yacht Club's inside course. There was a difference this year in racing form. No longer would the two yachts start from anchor position. Instead they would be given flying starts.

A dozen excursion steamers had come to the race course that day, plus a dozen yachts and even more sloops, to watch the racing. Designer Cuthbert was sailing master of the challenger. *Madeleine* was sailed by her own captain.

The two boats moved about, behind the starting line, jockeying for position as they waited for the starting gun. Captain Cuthbert was in a good position as the gun sounded—he was ahead and in the windward position as the start was signalled. Instead of moving across the line and taking the lead, as all who watched expected, he bore away and let the American defender slip in to windward of him.

The Countess of Dufferin was quickly blanketed from the wind by the *Madeleine,* and when two boats crossed the line, the *Madeleine* was seen to be ahead by a full 35 seconds.

The boats crossed on the port tack. *Madeleine* was flying her boom foresail and no jib-topsail. *The Countess of Dufferin* flew a lug foresail and a jib topsail. The captains then began to toy with their sails a bit, but it made no difference what they did—*Madeleine* was ahead and kept drawing away. Experienced sailors, who had taken close looks at both yachts, said that *The Countess of Dufferin* did not have much of a chance from the beginning because of her rough bottom and badly fitting sails. But she did have something of a chance, however this was lost for the first race in that bad start.

Madeleine gained all the way. At the Narrows the two boats passed on opposite tacks, the *Madeleine* ahead by an eighth of a mile. At the end of the first leg, *Madeleine* was more than 7 minutes ahead. They turned then parallel to the Long Island shore and by careful sailing, while *Madeleine* overstood the mark, *The Countess of Dufferin* picked up valuable time and was only 4 minutes and 41 seconds behind at the turn.

On the run home, the two yachts were closely followed by the excursion steamers and pleasure boats that hoped that the Canadian might catch up and make a closer race of it, but she did not. The *Madeleine* had it all her own way, and even though she lost time by passing too close under the Staten Island bluffs and losing the wind, she still finished almost 10 minutes ahead of the Canadian challenger. With all the corrections made for time (*Madeleine* had a slight handicap advantage because of her lesser weight) *Madeleine* was given the victory by 10 minutes and 59 seconds.

As suggested by the New York Yacht Club committee, this year the second race was outside, 20 miles to windward and back. There was more interest in this race than there had been in the first, because the old *America* had come up to New York again, with a full racing crew. She was not officially in the race, but she was welcomed to come along and race the course with the other two yachts, provided she started after they and stayed out of the way so as to create a nuisance.

For this day's race the Candians secured the services of Captain Joe Ellsworth, one of the New York's best-known yachting skippers.

The second race was sailed the next day. *Madeleine* had the better start and led *The Countess of Dufferin* across the line by 34 seconds. (*America* came along 4½ minutes later so as not to be in the way.) This course was sailed from Sandy Hook to the east, and while all three boats sailed fast, *The Countess of Dufferin* sagged down to leeward, while the *America* passed her and led her at the turn around the mark for the homeward course. *Madeleine* was in front, leading *America* by 3 minutes, and *The Countess of Dufferin* by 12 minutes.

On the run home the wind died out for a time, and all three yachts slowed, spreading every piece of canvas they could possibly stick on with rigging to catch the fading breeze. It was dark when they finally finished that day—*Madeleine* first, *America* behind by 12 minutes, and *The*

Countess of Dufferin behind *America* by 19 minutes. Again the defense had been made, by not one but two American defenders, although, *America's* part in the race was totally unofficial.

Following this race the New York Yacht Club set out on its annual cruise, inviting *The Countess of Dufferin*. Major Gifford and Captain Cuthbert decided against it—the fact was that they were having difficulties among themselves.

The Countess of Dufferin was laid up in the Seawanhaka basin at Staten Island and was stripped of her rigging there. After a few weeks when she was not returned to Canada there came rumors that the owners were in financial trouble.

She has been financed by a syndicate which included a large number of investors, and when the races had proved so unsatisfactory tempers grew short. Major Gifford and Captain Cuthbert could not agree on what was to be done with her. The designer took the case to court and had the boat attached, in an attempt to force Major Gifford to sell his interest in her, since Cuthbert was one of the largest shareholders. He thought he could strengthen the yacht and increase her speed by altering her stern, moving her rudder further aft, and shifting the masts. Then he wanted to challenge for The America's Cup once again.

The Countess of Dufferin remained in drydock on Staten Island for almost an entire year. Then, on July 27, 1877, another claimant came forward with a demand for $304 for the board of some of her crew while they were in New York. The sheriff advertised her for sale, and the centerboard boat was taken into New York waters across the bay. Actually she was more or less broken up—her sails were left in Staten Island to be sold to pay other debts.

Eventually *The Countess of Dufferin* was taken to Canada (some say she was stolen one night out of the sheriff's custody and sailed there). Eventually she made her way to Chicago and was purchased by S.C. Griggs, Jr., of the Chicago Yacht Club, who refitted her, charged her name to *The Countess,* and took her cruising around Lake Michigan. There she sailed very creditably in a number of races, but never again for The America's Cup.

Captain Cuthbert was disappointed, but he did not give up his hopes that he would again race for The America's Cup. He was certain that he knew how to design a yacht to win that trophy against any American comer. He had considerable confidence in the yacht, for he had designed her himself, and he was certain that the indifferent workmanship that had gone into her, because of the lack of funds from the beginning, had been the most serious difficulty with the poor *The Countess of Dufferin*. He returned to Canada, and set about planning to make another try for The Cup. It was five years before anything came of it, but no one else was interested. The British yachtsmen still smarted under the rules established by the New York Yacht Club and had no interest in challenging for The Cup.

5

The Competition Grows Fierce

In 1881 Alexander Cuthbert succeeded in finding the backing he needed to design and race a new yacht for what he called the famous "mug." In the spring of that year he began construction of a centerboard sloop which was to be christened *Atalanta*.

Cuthbert was then a member of a small yacht club on Lake Ontario called the Quinte Yacht Club, and it was from this club that challenge came. It was late—the six month's notice must again be waived if the challenge was to be made that year—but the New York Yacht Club was willing to waive the notice.

Once again came the inevitable discussions about the manner in which the cup would be defended. The Canadians wanted to know how many races the Americans would make, and how they would go about choosing their defenders. Without waiting to discover the answers to these questions, some Canadian newspapers began to criticize the New York Yacht Club for what were assumed to be its tactics: choosing a defender on the day of each race, depending on weather and sailing conditions to determine whether or not to use a centerboard boat or a keel boat. In the United States, newspapers began to criticize those in the yacht club who held out for a liberalization of the rules of defense.

The critics of both sides had their say, and the yacht club officials did what they thought best. This year they notified the Canadians that they would choose a single defender and she would sail all the races. No one could have asked for more.

All spring and summer the designer and workmen labored over the *Atalanta*. She was supposed to be ready in summer, but she was delayed in construction and was not finished until September 17. There was scarcely time to try her out before she must go to New York, if the races were to be held at all that year.

The challenge by a sloop posed new problems for the defending New York Yacht Club. All the fine racing yachts of the club were schooners because the sloop was a new type of boat and had not yet caught on in American yachting circles. In all the New York Yacht Club fleet there were only five sloops that might even be considered for defense of the cup against the new challenger. They were the *Hildegarde, Fanny, Vision, Gracie,* and *Mischief.*

The officers of The America's Cup committee went to see David Kirby, designer of the *Madeleine.* They asked him to build a sloop that would be faster than the *Madeleine* and faster than the *Arrow,* a very fast sloop that he had built for a yachtsman who was not a member of the New York Club. The request was made in the spring, and work was hastened so that the new yacht, the *Pocahontas,* would be ready for racing by October.

But when October came the *Atalanta* had still not arrived in New York. She was sent down to New York by way of the Erie Canal. The idea was to save time. But the *Atalanta's* beam was too broad to permit passage through the canal. The crew finally got her through by shifting her ballast and listing her to one side, and tying the mast and spars on deck as they went through the narrow locks.

She arrived in New York on October 30, several weeks after the end of the normal racing season.

While the passage of the *Atalanta* was carefully reported in the newspapers, the Americans who would defend The Cup were making their preparations.

By October 13 the *Pocahontas* was launched and ready, so a race was held to try her out. She was to race *Mischief, Gracie,* and *Hildegard,* to decide which yacht would defend The Cup for the United States.

In the first of these trials the wind was brisk; *Gracie* and *Pocahontas* lost their topmasts in going through the Narrows with its treacherous winds, and *Mischief* won the race.

Nearly a week was allowed for the crippled yachts to make their repairs. The second trial was held on October 19, with only *Gracie, Pocahontas* and *Mischief* starting. This time *Gracie* won, by barely 4 minutes. It was most disappointing, for the new yacht *Pocahontas* was far out of the running.

The Cup Committee had held great hopes for *Pocahontas.* They had really wanted to buy the *Arrow* in the beginning, for this sloop, which was owned by Ross Winans of Baltimore, was regarded as the speediest boat of her class in American waters. The committee had learned that Winans was in Europe and had considered cabling him to see if he would sell the yacht, when designer David Kirby promised them that he could build a much faster boat.

Pocahontas was given one more try. The three sloops raced again on

Atalanta

Mischief

October 20, and *Mischief* defeated *Gracie* by 14 seconds, which was as close as anyone could wish. Poor *Pochontas* was disabled again, and in disgust she was towed to her dock and stripped of her rigging, not to be commissioned again for the races.

The racing committee was faced with a most difficult decision. Which defender should they choose? Both boats had their advocates and both had their good points. *Gracie* and *Mischief* had each won a race, close as they were, and it was true that *Mischief* had finished first in the earliest contest, but *Gracie's* backers said this would never have happened had it not been for the sheer accident of the topmast stays failing when *Gracie* was actually in the lead.

No matter which decision they made the members of the committee were going to be criticized, and they knew it. For this reason, and for no other, they delayed deciding which boat would defend the cup until *Atalanta* arrived.

The Canadian challenger arrived on October 30. It took a bit of time to get her in shape for a contest—the first race was scheduled for November 8. When the weather proved foggy and windless the race was set over another day.

No decision about the defender was made until the morning of the race, and then it was announced that *Mischief* would defend officially for the New York Yacht Club because she had won two races to *Gracie's* one.

Mischief was 67 feet long with a beam of slightly less than 20 feet. She was a centerboard sloop with a draft of 5 feet, 4 inches. She was built of iron and was called "The Iron Pot" in yacht club circles.

The *Atalanta* was 70 feet long but had less beam to her, being nearly a foot narrower. She drew 5 feet, 6 inches of water. In those days the Americans raced with professional sailing crews, as did the yachtsmen of some other nations, particulary when competing. The Canadians did not. They brought with the *Atalanta* an amateur crew of yachting enthusiasts from Lake Ontario. Instead of hailing these amateur sailors because they were amateurs, New Yorkers tended to jeer at them because they were not nearly as adept at handling sails and rigging as were the professional sailors who manned the American yachts.

The race was sailed on November 9, when *Mischief* was announced as the defender. So great was the disappointment of the backers of *Gracie* that the club agreed to let *Gracie* make the run and to time her, although her performance would have no effect on the outcome of the contest between the defender and the challenger.

The course was to be the inside one of the yacht clubs, running down through the Narrows from Stapleton, Staten Island, and then back again.

There were not many spectators on hand on November 9, for the sailing season was long past, and the harbor was inclined to be unpleasantly windy and choppy.

Still, one of the Iron Steamboat Company's sidewheelers was on hand to follow the racers and carry an excursion group. A dozen tugs came along, and some 20 yachts and small boats of the New York Yacht Club were out to lend support to the racers.

The wind at the start was from the west-southwest, and the tide was just ending its flood. The defender and the challenger were given the signal to start at 11 minutes past 11 in the morning, and went over the line on the starboart tack—*Mischief* pulled into the lead immediately. Ten minutes later, *Gracie* set out, also being timed by the judges.

Mischief drew away from *Atalanta* steadily, and it was not long before *Gracie* came up and passed the Canadian entry, too. Before the three yachts reached the marker of the course, the knowledgeable yachtsmen could tell that *Atalanta* was no match for either of the American vessels.

From this first buoy to the finish, the real race was between the two American sloops. *Atalanta* was so far astern that she was out of it altogether. In the end *Mischief* beat *Atalanta* by 28½ minutes, but *Gracie,* when the corrected time was given, defeated *Mischief* by 6 minutes and 27 seconds. Of course there was nothing official about the *Gracie-Mischief* race except that it rubbed salt into the wounds of the poor Canadians—the official defender was not even the fastest boat on the water that day.

The following day the second race was held, this one out in open water on the outer course. The course was set at 16 miles, to leeward and return, which meant a fast sail out and beating back against the wind.

In the beginning *Atalanta* held her own with *Mischief* and as long as they sailed with the wind she handled well and at the turn was only a little over 2 minutes behind. But on the windward she began to lose, largely because of the inexperience of her crew, according to yachtsmen who watched the race that day.

Again *Atalanta* was defeated, but on this day *Mischief* had her revenge against her American rival. She defeated *Gracie's* time, when corrected, by about 4½ minutes.

Cuthbert was seriously disappointed because he had truly expected to win The America's Cup this year with his yacht. Americans laughed merrily at the thought; they regarded the *Atalanta* as more of a joke than a yacht. One newspaper had this to say:

"Divested of all sensational international claptrap, the race on Wednesday—if race it can be called—amounts to this: The *Mischief,* a tried and proved sloop, confessedly one of the fastest in the world, thoroughly fitted and equipped, fully manned and magnificently handled, distanced the *Atalanta,* a new yacht, hastily built, totally untried, and miserably equipped, with sails which misfitted like a Chatham street suit of clothes, and bungled around the course by an alleged crew, who would have been over-matched in trying to handle a canal boat anchored in a fog—only this and nothing more."

It was quite apparent that if the New York Yacht Club was willing to compromise and was showing the higher forms of sportsmanship, the New York public was not yet ready to play the gentleman's game.

Challenger Cuthbert wanted to try again. He laid the *Atalanta* up in New York with hopes of coming back and challenging again the next year after refitting.

Nothing was to come of that idea however, because the grumbling in the New York Yacht Club became so severe. The grumbling was over the waste of time and especially of money in preparing for a cup defense against so badly matched a competitor as *Atalanta.* The club's members had put up $20,000 for the building of the *Pocahontas;* they would never have done so had they not felt it necessary to put forth their best efforts in defense of the cup. To have the challenger appear and make so little contest caused many of those who had spend their money to complain.

Feeling grew very strong at the yacht club that the entire spirit of The America's Cup competition, as envisaged by the original winners of the cup, had been violated by the last two challenges. In both cases the challenger was ill-equipped, financially weak, and the crews not properly trained to give a first-class run in the badly finished yacht the Canadians had entered.

This attitude was predominant in the winter of that year, 1881, when at a meeting of the club it was voted to return the cup to George Schuyler, the surviving member of the old syndicate, and ask him to draw up a new deed of gift which would protect the club from having to defend against anyone who felt inpelled to challenge.

The new deed of gift set forth many of the old conditions, but added several to prevent repetition of the *Atalanta* incident. First was the provision that no challenger could repeat his challenge after defeat until another challenger had come between, or two years had passed. Second was a provision that all vessels intending to challenge must sail from their home ports to the place where the race would be held. And it was distinctly stated that The Cup, no matter who won it, would become the property of the yacht club challenging, and not the property of any individual, and that it would always be available in the future for challenge by other nations, no matter who won. The deed also put in writing the new custom of choosing a single defender.

In the late winter of 1882 the New York Yacht Club accepted the new deed of gift and caused copies of it to be sent to all the foreign yacht clubs it recognized and wished to encourage, and promised anyone who might challenge a hearty welcome and strict fair play. Still, so serious was the rift of a few years before that three years went by before any British yachtsman would give serious consideration to a contest with the Americans.

6

The Boston "Bean Boat"

In December, 1884, the officers of the New York Yacht Club had word that in the near future they would have not one, but two challenges for The America's Cup by cutters designed by the English naval architect, J. Beavor Webb.

Here was the proposal, when it came: Sir Richard Sutton challenged with his *Genesta,* asking that three races be run over the outside course. If he lost the challenge, then another, the *Galatea* wanted to race a second series over the same course. Like the *Genesta,* the *Galatea* was a cutter—a small craft much like a sloop except that a sloop's mast was placed further forward than a cutter's and the sloop carried one mainsail and two foresails, or jib, while the cutter carried a mainsail and one basic foresail, or jib, while the cutter carried a mainsail and two foresails, one above the other. These, of course, were basic sails. To catch more wind a topsail could be placed above the mainsail, which gave the craft four large spreads of canvas to be used in favorable winds.

The New York Yacht Club accepted the challenge, although it meant the club would have to defend twice in the same season if its defender won the first series of races.

At this time the British designers were working very successfully with a new type of sailing yacht. The first of these was the *Vanduara,* a 90 ton cutter launched in 1880. She was followed by others, each growing a little longer and a little narrower. These craft were known as "plank-on-edge" vessels, the term describing their general appearance. They were much faster than earlier varieties of cutters and sloops because they carried their ballast very low in the water as compared to the older types of vessels.

In 1881 the Americans had been introduced to these swift cutters when a Scotch cutter named *Madge* was shipped to the United States aboard a steamer by her owner and raced in the waters of the east coast. She was 46 feet long, but had a beam of only 7 feet, 9 inches, which made her very narrow by the standards of that day. She was deep, drawing nearly 8 feet of water. *Madge* raced so successfully wherever she went that soon yachtsmen began to argue the merits of cutters as opposed to the old centerboard sloops, and it was not long before a new variety of sloop was developed which had some characteristics of both types (American and English).

The members of the New York Club surveyed the American vessels that might be able to defend The Cup against the English challengers and found none that would be suitable, so they began counseling among themselves. Commodore James Gordon Bennett and vice-commodore William Douglas approached A. Cary Smith, America's foremost designer, and asked him to build them a sloop that could match the English cutters in speed. Smith had designed *Mischief,* the last cup defender, so he was the logical man for them to seek.

Designer Smith suggested that they build a compromise sloop, a centerboard vessel, but one with a deep draft, and much narrower than the usual run of such yachts. The officials of the club agreed, and the yacht's plans were sent to the yard of Harlan and Hollingsworth in Wilmington, Delaware. When she was finished, she was christened *Priscilla.*

There was nothing in the rules of the New York Yacht Club which said that the defender of The America's Cup must be chosen by the commodore of the club or any of the officers. At that particular time sailing had become much more popular in the United States than in the past, and a number of yacht clubs in the Boston area had become active in racing with clubs up and down the coast. Members of the Eastern Yacht Club at Marblehead, Massachusetts, decided they could form a syndicate, build a yacht, and attempt to win the honor of defending The America's Cup. Leaders of this syndicate were General Charles J. Paine and Malcolm Forbes. The general was also a member of the New York Yacht Club, so there could be no complaint that outsiders were trying to take control.

In Boston at that time there lived a young sailing enthusiast named Edward Burgess who had taught himself something about naval architecture and had designed a number of small boats which had turned out to be quite successful. The largest of these was only 38 feet, but so well did they sail that he had acquired a considerable reputation in New England as a designer.

The Eastern Yacht Club syndicate sought him out and asked him to design a boat to defend The Cup, and also to compete with *Priscilla.*

Burgess' overall plan seemed very much like that of a cutter. The boat was built of wood, with a high freeboard and other characteristics of the English design. Her breadth of beam, however, was taken from the

American sloop plan. She was given more draft than the old "skimmer" sloops, but less than the usual cutter. She had a very definite keel that was about 2 feet deep, and the slot for the centerboard was cut through this keel. She was a big boat, 81 feet long at the waterline, but with much overhang which made her 94 feet overall. Her beam was 22 feet, 7 inches wide and she drew 8 feet, 8 inches of water, but 20 feet when her centerboard was down.

The *Priscilla,* when finished, was 94 feet overall, 22 feet, 5 inches wide, and 7 feet 9 inches in draft. The *Genesta,* the challenger, was 90 feet overall, but only 15 feet wide and she drew 13 feet, 6 inches of water. She also had 72 tons of lead ballast in her keel.

The second challenger, *Galatea,* was 102 feet long, with a beam of 15 feet and a draft of 13 feet, 6 inches. *Galatea,* however, sent word well before the season began that she would withdraw from the competition for 1885 and would challenge in 1886 if the *Genesta* did not win the cup away from the Americans.

So it was apparent that the contest would be between two types of yachts as well as two nationalities, and this suited the yachting world very well, because the argument was then raging as to the attributes of the cutter versus the sloop.

New Yorkers were very much interested in the *Priscilla,* but they paid no attention to reports of the prowess of the *Puritan,* even after she was launched in May, 1885. When they spoke of her at all, it was to call her the "bean boat" or the "brick sloop." Then the "bean boat" left Boston and came down to New York to enjoy the racing season.

Puritan and *Priscilla* were both scheduled to race in another race early in August. When the *Puritan* appeared in New York she had already won several races for the season. She had sailed in the Eastern Yacht Club regatta on June 30, competing with several sloops and cutters, and winning over all of them by half an hour or more on a 30-mile course. Not only that, she beat out four schooners, including the old *America,* original winner of the cup. Had the New Yorkers been less supercilious, they would have looked *Puritan* over more closely than they did. They were supremely confident in their *Priscilla,* and so it was a very great shock when the Boston boat came home a winner, leading *Priscilla* handily by more than 10 minutes. She raced *Priscilla* twice more during the New York Yacht Club's cruise, and of the three, *Puritan* won two. Then came the serious trials for the honor of defending the cup. *Gracie* was entered, and so was a sloop named *Bedouin.* *Puritan* defeated them all, including *Priscilla,* winning two of the three races handily and showing herself by far the most superior American boat in sailing to windward.

On August 30, eight days before The America's Cup races were scheduled to begin, the committee named *Puritan* as the American defender, much to the delight of the Massachusetts yachtsmen.

Genesta, the British challenger, arrived in New York on July 16 with a fine reputation behind her and a good passage across the Atlantic. It had taken her 24 days. She was kept quite out of sight and out of racing, because the challengers did not want to give the Americans any inkling of the manner in which she handled or her speed.

The Americans had already heard of her speed and her superior performance as an all-around yacht. In the season of 1884, *Genesta* had shown how well she could do. Her first race, being from Southend to Harwich, was at the regatta of the New Thames Yacht Club on May 31, 1884. *Genesta* won this contest by 2 minutes and 55 seconds against *Vanduara's* second. That latter yacht had been considered the year before as a possible contender for The America's Cup.

On June 2, 1884, *Genesta* had raced in the Royal Harwich Yacht Club regatta for a 50-mile course, and once again won. The next day she defeated the field again, winning against the *Miranda,* Britain's fastest two-masted schooner, as well as against the cutters.

Later in the season she raced in the Royal Cinque Ports Yacht Club regatta and across the tricky English channel from Dover to Boulogne. During the season she won 7 first and 10 second places in 34 starts, which made her one of two outstanding yachts in England for the year, the other being the *Tara,* who started 35 times and won 19 firsts and 4 seconds.

Late in the summer *Genesta* went into drydock. She came out on September 2, and no one among the New York Yacht Club membership could complain that they were not getting competition this year from a well-found and well-rigged yacht. She had been freshly coppered and hand polished until a man could see his reflection in her. Lapthorn, the English sailmaker, had come over with the boat to give the sails and rigging his full attention right up to the last moment. There was no complaint about the way her sails fit or how they handled.

The first race was scheduled to be held on September 7. On that day, as the two racing yachts lay at anchor, there were many who were willing to wager that the slim, sleek *Genesta* would win over the *Puritan.* She looked every inch a racer, and a champion, as her black hull glistened in the water.

The morning of September 7 dawned, and with it came a low lying fog that blanketed New York Harbor. Even so, a crowd of excursion steamers and yachts followed the officials to the starting line to watch the two

Genesta

Spectators' boat at the *America's* Cup race, 1885.

yachts in what promised to be a great race. The crowd was disappointed that day. The fog was less on the outside course, which was to be the race course, but there was so little wind that after delaying the race for several hours the officials finally postponed it until the following day.

September 8 was a beautiful day for racing. The sky was clear and blue and the sun was shining brightly, and most important, there was a steady brisk wind blowing.

The readiness signal was given at 11:32 that morning and both yachts began to move toward the starting line. They came up first with *Puritan* on the port tack and *Genesta* on the starboard tack. Captain Aubrey Crocker of *Puritan* tried to cross *Genesta's* bows as they came to the line, either attempting to bluff the British captain into going about, rather than risk a collision, or miscalculating the distance and the speed. The British challenger, on the starboard tack, had the right-of-way. At the last moment it was apparent on the American yacht that she could not clear the challenger, so the helmsman luffed across the *Genesta's* bow, pulling back into the wind, in order to avoid the collision. It was too late. The *Genesta's* bowsprit crashed through the *Puritan's* tearing a huge rent in the sail, but snapping off her bowsprit, too.

There was no question about the fault of this accident. *Puritan* was definitely at fault for not yielding the right-of-way to the boat on the starboard tack, and the officials in the committee boat immediately disqualified the defender. All the British challenger had to do to win the race was to go ahead and sail the course within the 7 hours given as an outside time for making a race, and they would automatically be awarded the first race. Sir Richard Sutton, owner of *Genesta*, was so informed, but he said he had to race and not to be awarded victories on fouls, and he refused to continue the race. He said that after the damage to the boats was repaired it should be resailed.

This was the greatest generosity and the finest sportsmanship that had been shown by any yachtsman to date in The America's Cup races, which until this time had been better known for bad sportsmanship than for good. When Sir Richard's remarks were made known to the press and then to people all over America, the popularity of the challengers became immense, and the interest in the cup races increased considerably.

It was three days before the damage caused by *Puritan* was repaired and both boats were ready for racing again. There was a light east wind on September 11, quite enough for starting, and the two yachts set out over the course 20 miles to windward and return. But very shortly after the two vessels started at 11:35 in the morning, the wind began to die, and it was 6 hours before *Puritan* rounded the buoy at the far end of the course with *Genesta* about a mile astern. It was apparent that neither vessel could finish within the time limit of seven hours, consequently the race was called off again.

The third attempt began on the morning of September 14 in a good southwest wind. This time the yachts sailed the club's inside course. *Puritan* gained the advantage in the beginning as *Genesta* was carried to leeward by a strong flood tide. Then, in beating down the bay, *Genesta* was troubled by a ship that was coming into the New York Harbor through the Narrows. This was to be expected as part of the luck of racing, and there was no complaint when *Genesta* fell back about 7 minutes behind *Puritan*, by the time they reached Fort Wadsworth. The challenger worked well in the uncertain winds the yachts met in the lower bay, and on the next leg she gained 4 minutes. The following leg was to sail to the lightship, and on this portion, reaching, or sailing at right angles to the wind, the challenger was crowded by watchers in their excursion boats, and the wash of some of the steamers affected her progress. This was very annoying to the crew of the British vessel, and it definitely hampered her progress. *Puritan* was ahead by nearly 4½ minutes at the halfway point of the race. Perhaps *Genesta* could have made up some or all of this, but the wind began to die down, and she kept dropping behind, so that she was about a mile astern as *Puritan* crossed the finish line. By anyone's measure it was a bad ending to the race, with neither vessel able to show flash or spirit in the dying breeze. *Puritan,* then, had won the first contest.

The second race was sailed on September 16, and for once the wind was strong and the day was fine for racing. It was the outside course again, with a northwest wind blowing, which gave the two yachts a straight run downwind for the first half of the course, with a beat against the wind to get home. *Genesta* was ahead at the start by 45 seconds, and she had her spinnaker up and her big topsail billowing. She continued to open the gap between herself and *Puritan*, until she reached the turn, where she was well ahead. As she turned into the wind to begin beating back for the second half of the course, her crew took in the big topsail and set a small gaff topsail in its place, a sail much easier to handle in tacking.

The *Puritan* did the same, except that after taking in her topsail, she housed her topmast, and sailed without extra canvas. The *Genesta* had too much canvas up for a wind that was growing steadily stronger. She lay over heavily in the breeze as she sailed, and while this was an exciting scene to the spectators, it slowed her seriously as she moved into the wind, and tended to push her away from the points at which she was aiming in her zig-zag course to sail home. *Puritan,* sailing close before the wind with less canvas, and sailing a course of much smaller angles, was catching up all the time, and caught up shortly before the finish. Then it was a close finish, with the two yachts roaring through the wind and water, keeling over and water rushing along the lee rails. *Puritan* came stronger at the end, passed *Genesta* and led her across the finish line in a great burst of speed as the wind changed to let the yachts sail a reach. The corrected time of *Puritan* was 5:03:14. That of *Genesta* was 5:04:52.

That race ended the series. The losers came up alongside the winning *Puritan* and gave three cheers, ending the most satisfactory and sportsmanlike series that had ever been sailed for The America's Cup.

Sir Richard Sutton remained in the United States for several weeks, seeking other races. He tried to arrange another race against the *Puritan,* but the owners realized that if they won they could not gain anything and if they lost some would always question the *Puritan's* clean victory in The Cup races. So there was no further contest between the two cup racers, but *Genesta* did win the Bennett and Douglas cups and also the Brenton and Cape May Challenge cups in the next few weeks. She went home with many honors, if not the ones she came to win.

Puritan was sold that autumn to J. Malcolm Forbes, a New Yorker, who kept her for many years as his private yacht, sailing her both as a sloop and as a schooner. In 1905 she was sold to an owner who lived in the Cape Verde Islands and was sailed in the Atlantic for a number of years thereafter.

7

The Era of Good Feeling

In 1886 the officers of the New York Yacht Club received the expected challenge from the Royal Northern Yacht Club of Scotland on behalf of Lieutenant William Henn's *Galatea*, a yacht that had also been built by Beavor Webb, the man who made *Genesta*.

Galatea represented something new in yacht design, for she was built of steel. She was 102 feet long, with a beam of 15 feet and a draft of more than 13 feet long, slim, deep—a typical Webb pattern—she also carried 81 tons of ballast in her keel.

When the challenge was received, General Paine of Boston regarded himself and his syndicate of New Englanders as the men to meet it, since they had backed *Puritan,* which had walked away from the New Yorkers' *Priscilla.* If the cup was to be defended successfully, it seemed likely to them that they would have to do it, hence the general placed an order with Edward Burgess for a new sloop.

Burgess designed a new yacht, which would be called the *Mayflower.* She had the same general configuration as *Puritan*—deep hull, lead ballast fixed outside the keel, an overhanging stern, and a rigging that was copied from the cutter rig, with some modification. She was 100 feet long on deck tapering down to 85½ feet at the waterline, making 16 inches shorter there than *Galatea.*

Mayflower was much broader in the beam than *Galatea.* She measured 23½ feet across, and her draft was only 9 feet, 9 inches, although with her centerboard down she drew 20 feet. She carried about 250 more feet of sail than *Galatea's* 7751 square feet.

When the New Yorkers heard that the New Englanders were building they quickly changed their plans. They had hoped to improve *Priscilla* enough to use her as defender this year, but with the announcement that the general had commissioned a new boat, they also commissioned a sloop to be built, which was to be called the *Atlantic.*

Galatea

Animals on *Galatea*

General Charles J. Paine

Puritan

There was another complication among the defenders, or potential defenders, in 1886. The New York owners of *Puritan* did not feel that she was out of the running simply because she had defended once, and during the summer races of the yachting season her owners set out to prove the point. General Paine brought his new *Mayflower* to race with *Puritan,* and lost the first three races. The New Yorkers were just congratulating themselves on bringing the defense back to their own waters when the Goelet Cup races were held in August, and *Mayflower* beat *Puritan* by 6 minutes on a 40 mile course, and then proceeded to win every other race she entered.

Galatea arrived in American waters on August 1, after leisurely cruising across the Atlantic, and joined the New York Yacht Club fleet on its outing in Buzzard's Bay. A number of yachtsmen wanted to challenge her when they saw her sailing, but Lietutenant Henn always towed a dinghy astern, to show that he was not in a race, and thus to keep the snoopers from discovering *Galatea's* strengths and weaknesses.

On August 21, the trials began for the selection of the official Cup defender of 1886. *Mayflower, Atlantic, Puritan,* and *Priscilla* all competed, but it was really no competition, since *Mayflower* won the first race by 10 minutes and the second by 4 minutes.

The races began on September 7 to decide who would have this year's America's Cup. In the first race, over the inside course of the New York Yacht Club, *Galatea* managed a fine start, blanketing the American defender with her big sails, and thus cutting off part of the wind from the defender. It took Captain Henry Haff two tacks to escape from the trap. At any time, of course, he could have fallen off or steered wide in order to escape from the wind interference of the British challenger, but in doing so would have given the other yacht the advantage of a straighter, shorter course, however the Americans might have lost the race by using that strategy.

Having escaped the blanketing, *Mayflower* began to draw ahead of the challenger, which was expected by the yachting enthusiasts among the American crowd, because by now they were very much convinced of the superiority of the centerboard in working to windward. At the halfway point, *Mayflower* had managed to move 4 minutes ahead, and when the two yachts came back with the wind, spinnakers ballooning ahead of them, she won the race by more than 12 minutes, after the *Galatea* was given the agreed time allowance of 38 seconds.

Two days later, when the second race was to be held, the wind failed and the contest was delayed until September 11, this time over the outer course, as was usual. *Mayflower* drew ahead quickly, but before the race was halfway along, the wind began to fail and on the homeward course it died out completely for hours. Finally a few snatches of breeze came along from the Jersey shore which made a race of it. *Mayflower* was able to cross the finish line 11 minutes before the 7-hour time limitation, with *Galatea* half hour later.

That was the end of The America's Cup defense of 1886, with the defender having won two straight races. The challengers took the defeat squarely, but Lieutenant Henn said he felt that the weather had not been proper for his boat this season, and he suggested, just for his own satisfaction, a race in a real breeze out at sea.

They raced off Marblehead—or they were supposed to. Lieutenant Henn sailed *Galatea* up into Massachusetts waters, and the two yachts lay still for 10 days waiting for a breeze that never came.

The following spring *Mayflower* and *Galatea* did arrange to run a race which was held in the strong breeze in which Lieutenant Henn thought *Galatea* could show her best. *Mayflower* won again, and this time Lieutenant Henn was satisfied that the American defender was indeed the better boat.

In the fall of 1886, shortly after the end of the *Galatea-Mayflower* races, the officers of the New York Yacht Club received a letter from the Royal Clyde Yacht Club of Scotland, proposing a race in the summer of 1887 by James Bell with a yacht which would be about the size as the *Mayflower*.

For some reason this offhand suggestion annoyed someone in the New York Yacht Club and a stiff and notably unfriendly note was returned to the Royal Clyde Club, pointing out that the challenge was to be made 6 months in advance but not more than 7 months in advance, and that when the challenge was presented in proper form it would be duly considered. On this note the gentlemen of the Royal Clyde Yacht Club were annoyed, however they tried again to discover if the Americans would agree to certain general size stipulations regarding yachts to be raced. The point was that the British intended to build a yacht to challenge, and did not want to build one and then have the Americans build another to such a different design that the race would be between incomparable craft. For the first time, in other words, the challengers were building a special boat, and so the question of being outbuilt occurred to them.

The Royal Clyde Club never did get any clarification about the building of the yachts, and so the plans had to be made without advance knowledge. The response of the challengers was to adhere strictly to the letter of the rules of challenge and to give out no more than the minimum

Mayflower

Thistle

Gen. Paine, Capt. Stone, and J. Beavor-Webb

Volunteer

information about the challenger. In due time the challenge was sent officially. It named the yacht *Thistle.* It gave her waterline length at 85 feet. That was all.

The designer of *Thistle* was Geroge L. Watson, the man who had built *Madge,* the little cutter which had gone to America to win so many races and cause the change of design of racing sloops there. *Thistle* was built to an even more advanced design. She was made very broad for a cutter, more than 20 feet wide as compared to 108 feet long on deck. She sloped radically into the water both fore and aft. Noting that the American yachts of the past had always carried more canvas than the challengers, she was to carry 8968 feet of canvas.

The challenge was issued in March, but when it came with so little information about the British boat, the Americans were concerned and puzzled. Within the next 6 months they must build a new yacht or they must rely on one of their old ones. It seemed apparent that the challengers were trying something new, but all the Americans had to go on were the facts that the boat would be designed by the builder of *Madge,* and that she would be 85 feet long.

General Paine again offered to build a boat, and when he was encouraged to do so he took the problem to Edward Burgess.

The challenger was to be 85 feet long, so the defender, named *Volunteer,* would be nearly 86 feet long. That much could be coped with. She was also given more sail surface than any previous defender—9271 square feet. She had a 23 foot beam and a 10 foot draft, plus the length of the centerboard.

The English challenger was built in absolute secrecy, but she was launched in April and began competing in races in English waters. The results were not very comforting to the defenders, for of 15 races, *Thistle* won 11, took one second and one third. She defeated *Genesta* with ease when they met.

Thistle sailed to the United States in 22 days, arriving August 16. Shortly after she arrived, a diver went down below her one dark night to explore her bottom on behalf of a New York newspaper.

The interest in the lines and "secrets" of *Thistle* stemmed from the mutual irritations and suspicions created by the original challenge and testy American response. For the first time in this year, the two yachts that were to race had both been built specifically for the contest, which also created a new situation. Americans and Britons, it appeared, were both looking for an argument.

A cause was soon found. When *Thistle* was measured in water before the race, she was discovered to be 86.4 feet long at the waterline rather than 85 feet. This was quite readily understandable for she sloped away so rapidly, fore and aft, that an inch or two of extra immersion could mean a foot or two of extra length at the water line. The extra immersion could be caused by a slight increase in ballast.

The Americans did not know this, however, because the hull design of *Thistle* had been carefully kept from them, and was still secret at the time of the race. Some harsh words were said within the clubrooms of the New York Yacht Club, and for a time it appeared that the race might be called off. The dispute was finally referred to George Schuyler, the still surviving member of the original America's Cup winners. He took the calm view that the extra water length of the challenger would simply be settled, as usual, in the determination of time allowances by the accepted formula.

Most Americans accepted the *Volunteer* as the defender for the races that year, even without trials, but E.D. Morgan of the New York Yacht Club, who had purchased *Mayflower,* felt that the old defender ought to have her chance to win again, and so a single race was run for the honor of the defense. *Volunteer* won by more than 16 minutes.

The races for The Cup were set for September 27 and thereafter until two had been won by a contender.

The morning of the first race was foggy, and the breeze was light. The contenders moved back and forth waiting for the starting signal, while steamers and private yachts filled with watchers looked over the performance of the yachts and bet on the outcome of the races. *Thistle* seemed to have all the best of it, moving quickly and responding readily, while *Volunteer* seemed heavy and sluggish in comparison.

This year, 1887, the challengers felt they truly had the better boat, and the pre-race performances seemed to back up their contention.

The starting gun did not sound until after noon, and when it came both yachts were far back of the line. *Thistle* came across first, on the port tack, some 2 minutes ahead of *Volunteer,* in the south-southeast breeze. Less than 15 minutes after the start, *Volunteer* crossed the *Thistle's* bow in tacking, having made up the 2 minutes very quickly. The truth then began to dawn on the spectators. Captain Haff of the *Volunteer,* had been "dogging it" during those pre-race maneuvers, making his boat appear to be sluggish to beguile the challengers. By the time *Volunteer* reached the Spit Buoy and rounded it to head for the Sandy Hook Lightship, she was 15 minutes ahead. By the time *Volunteer* reached the lightship—the halfway mark—she was a mile ahead, and when she came home with the wind, she arrived at the finish line 20 minutes ahead of the challenger. The first race went to the defender.

James Bell, owner of the challenger, was so disappointed in the performance of *Thistle,* with which he had expected to win handily, that he refused to believe she had been beaten by a better yacht. He had *Thistle's* bottom inspected but found nothing wrong. He complained about the course, saying it was the worst course he had ever sailed, with its tricky tides and slack spots, and points against the shore where the yachts could be covered from the wind. This was true, but the *Volunteer* had sailed the same course.

The second race was to be sailed on a course 20 miles to windward and return, out at sea, from the Scotland Lightship. On September 29 the racers went outside the Narrows, but there was not enough wind, and so the race was not run until the following day.

Thistle was ahead at the start, once again, but she did not sail into the wind as well as *Volunteer*. She could not sail as close-pointed into the wind, which meant that she fell away from the mark and her angle of tack must be greater than *Volunteer's*. This was very noticeable on the run out, against the wind, for *Volunteer* passed *Thistle,* and turned around the marker at the halfway point nearly 14 minutes ahead of the challenger. *Thistle* began to pick up on the run back before the wind, her superior hull design showing, and she reduced the lead by 3 minutes, but the windward advantage was too great, and *Volunteer* won by more than 11 minutes, thus again successfully defending The Cup for America.

Thistle was sailed home to Britain. The next year she was sold to Kaiser Wilhelm of Germany, who renamed her the *Meteor* and raced her for several seasons with some success.

8

Racing Grows Complicated

After the races of 1887, the officers of the New York Yacht Club decided that the terms of The America's Cup races were becoming most difficult and unfavorable. There was a considerable amount of discontent about the British adherence to the letter of the challenge, in sending only the name and waterline length of the challenger, with even the latter stated inaccurately, as it turned out.

When the rules for the races were established, no one could foresee that special yachts would be built by one side or the other for challenges. Yacht design in the middle of the nineteenth century had been based on vessels used for far more pedestrian purposes than just racing. The *America*, for example, was designed after the fast pilot schooners which were used to cruise the inland waters of the American East Coast. But in a quarter of a century, on both sides of the Atlantic, yachting became a favorite rich man's sport, and so the whole approach to yachting was changed. With the German Kaiser in the yachting fraternity, and with many other wealthy men turning to the racing of small craft, it seemed quite logical for the New York Yacht Club to be deluged from all sides with challenges for The America's Cup. It was also becoming apparent that in each case new designs would be advanced, and that in nearly every defense a new yacht would have to be built to take advantage of new developments and design discoveries in yachting. With the growing expense of boat building, it became apparent that some limitations must be placed on the defense of The Cup, if matters were not to get out of hand.

So in October, 1887, the officers of the New York Yacht Club again returned The America's Cup to George L. Schuyler, and asked him to draw a more specific deed of gift. The new deed established definite waterline limitations on the yachts. If one mast, the yacht must be between 65 and 90 feet long; if two mast or more, it must be 80 feet to 115 feet.

The challenger must thereafter give 10 months notice, not 6. No races would be sailed between November 1 and May 1. The challenger must give the dimensions of his boat 10 months before the races. The parties could agree on the terms of races, but if they did not agree, then three races would be sailed, with the winners of two of them to hold the cup. All would be sailed over ocean courses, free from headlands, with the first race 20 miles windward and return, the second race over a triangular course, and the third, if necessary, as the first. Also, if the challenger and defender could not agree on terms, the challenger would have to race without any time allowance.

These changes were not altogether made to favor the American defenders. For many years the challengers had complained about the New York Yacht Club's inside course, and in this new set of rules that course was outlawed forever, because it ran between the headland of Brooklyn shore and Staten Island. The triangular course to be sailed in the second race also added another dimension. It tried the yachts under every sailing situation—tack, reach, run.

When the yacht clubs of Europe, and particularly of England, received the new set of rules for challenge, most of them complained that the rules were unfair. James Bell owner of the unsuccessful *Thistle*, had issued another challenge or announced his intention of doing so, however he withdrew his challenge with the statement that no Englishman would challenge under these conditions. The English did not like the change to 10 months notice, because it was too long a time. They did not like the demand that the challenger give dimensions 10 months ahead of the race. Among other things, they said, this was a demand that the challenger give up all his secrets while the defender revealed none of his. They did not like the clause which would force the challenger to sail without a time allowance unless the conditions of racing could be settled by agreement. Bell specifically said he would never give the dimensions of his yacht so far in advance of the race.

The officers of the New York Yacht Club had no intention of making it impossible for challengers to come forward, and they became concerned about the uproar which came from England. They referred the problem to George Schuyler, with particular reference to the matter of dimensions. He replied that he had really intended to place greatest importance on the matter of changing the courses, which was very much in favor of the challenger, by eliminating the old inside course of the yacht club.

But what Mr. Schuyler did not answer was the greatest objection of all: that if the exact dimensions were given, no racing yacht was allowed any margin for trimming, that is for adjusting ballast and position in the water so as to make the most speed.

The challengers, or potential challengers, said that it was practically impossible to design a racing boat that would float at her designed waterline and would be ready to race without changes.

No challenge at all was made then in 1888, and the outspoken British yachtsmen said no challenge would ever be made again. In the spring of 1889, however, the Royal Yacht Squadron did issue a challenge naming the Earl of Dunraven's *Valkyrie* as the yacht to race. It was stated that the waterline length of the boat would not exceed 70 feet, and that was all that was said. The New York Yacht Club was inclined to accept this part of the challenge, but in the correspondence they indicated that if the British won, they must continue to hold the cup in terms of the Deed of Gift, in which these new rules were set down. The British said they believed the rules were unfair and that they would not require others to race under them if they did win the cup. So the challenge of 1899 was withdrawn.

Three years went by, no challengers appeared. Then the Dunraven challenge was renewed; the New York Club agreed to waive the matter of overall dimensions except waterline length, and the Royal Yacht Squadron agreed to abide by the rules of the deed if they won the cup.

It was agreed that the new challenger would be Lord Dunraven's *Valkyrie II,* and that a best three-out-of-five races would be sailed for possession of The Cup, rather than the two of three that had been the custom in the past.

Valkyrie II was to be designed and built under the supervision of George L. Watson, the designer of the *Thistle,* who had exerted such a strong new force in yacht architecture. His ideas had come to the United States in the 1880's and had been seized upon by the Herreshoff family, boatbuilders of Bristol, Rhode Island, who had adapted them to American conditions and styles and had come up with a design for what was to be called the S-boat. Like the Watson yachts it had a long overhang, fore and aft, with very slight angle in the sweep from tip of stem or stemhead to the bottom of the keel. The yacht drew its type name from the look of her at the midship line—the curve was very nearly like that of an "S." The S-boats were much more extreme in design than anything produced by Watson or any other naval architect on either side of the Atlantic. The first was called the *Gloriana.* When she was launched yachtsmen came to laugh at her. When she was first raced and won, they said it was a fluke, but she won every race she entered that season, sailing far ahead of all comers.

A syndicate of members of the New York Yacht Club decided to advance the money to build a cup defender which would compete with the British yacht. They knew it must be a big yacht, which meant an

Valkyrie II

Nathanael Greene Herreshoff

expensive one. *Valkyrie II,* for example, carried more than 10,000 square feet of canvas, which was almost twice as much as the 5200 feet of the original *America.* Two grandsons of old Commodore Vanderbilt were among the syndicate, as was F.A. Schermerhorn, descendent of an old Dutch New York family and J. Pierpont Morgan, American representative of a banking firm born in England. The yacht was to be called the *Colonia* and she was to be built of steel.

General Paine's son John designed another sloop, *Jubilee,* for entry into the field. She was a steel boat of the fin-keel type, as opposed to the *Colonia,* a straight keelboat.

And in spite of the expense, about which the yachtsmen complained, there were two other candidates for the defense this year. One was a shallow fin-keel boat called *Pilgrim,* built by a Boston syndicate, and the other was *Vigilant,* built also by the Herreshoff yard for a second New York syndicate headed by C. Oliver Iselin. *Vigilant* was a deep centerboard boat, with a hull made of bronze.

These boats were ready for racing in the summer and created unusual interest in yachting and in the forthcoming cup races. By midsummer it was apparent that the two Boston yachts were outclassed by the Herreshoff vessels, because the Rhode Island sloops could sail much better into the wind. Still, the four boats raced in the trials, beginning on September 7. *Colonia* won the first race, beating *Vigilant* by 6 seconds. *Vigilant* won the second race by 4 minutes and 32 seconds, but in this race *Jubilee* was second, and *Colonia* was last. In the third race *Vigilant* again won by 6 minutes and 43 seconds, with *Colonia* second. The America's Cup committee then chose *Vigilant* to be the defender, and she was made ready for The Cup races, which would begin on October 5.

Vigilant was a larger boat than *Valkyrie II.* She was 124 feet long, overall, compared to *Valkyrie II's* 117 feet, although she was only 2 inches longer at waterline than *Valkyrie II's* 85 feet, 10 inches. *Vigilant's* beam was 26 feet wide, compared to *Valkyrie II's* 22 feet. She drew 14 feet, but when sailing into the wind could put down her bronze centerboard and add 10 feet to that draft. *Valkyrie II* drew 16 feet. *Vigilant* carried 1200 more feet of sail than *Valkyrie II.* Also, *Vigilant* carried a crew of 70, compared to *Valkyrie's* crew of 35.

In the first race, on October 5, *Valkyrie II* caught a breeze when a calm suddenly descended on *Vigilant,* and the challenger moved to a point 26 minutes ahead of the defender at the outer mark of the course. Then the wind died altogether, and the race could not be finished within the 7 hour time limit. It was called off, with the certain knowledge that *Valkyrie II* had been far ahead.

There was a change in the rules of racing this year which put a new value on skillful maneuvering at the start of a cup race. Much earlier the yachts had started from an anchor position. The rules had been changed some years after the beginning of the races so that the yachts maneuvered back and forth behind the starting line, then began the race at the sound of the gun. The first yacht to cross the line had an advantage, in that if both were on the same tack the first yacht might be able to blanket the second, but as far as time was concerned the second yacht's time began at that point where the yacht crossed the starting line, if the yacht crossed within 2 minutes. If the second yacht was so far back that it could not cross within 2 minutes, it was given 2 minutes of grace, and its starting time was counted from that point. Thus the yachts were really racing time far more than one another under the old system.

In this race of 1893 and thereafter, the gun that signalled the start also signalled the timing for both vessels, and so the sailors who could get their boat under way and settled were given an advantage at the beginning. Once again *Valkyrie II* got away first, but *Vigilant* caught her this time and passed her. She drew ahead to the outer mark, and there was 8 minutes and 6 seconds in the lead.

On the trip back, *Valkyrie II* gained, but not nearly enough, for at the end, even with an allowance of nearly 2 minutes, she was beaten by 5 minutes, 48 seconds.

The second race was sailed on October 9 over the new triangular course of three legs, each 10 miles long. The first of these was to be sailed into the wind, and the other two both called for reaching. *Vigilant* had the jump on the start and never lost the lead, keeping the challenger to the leeward and blanketing her for a time. At the first mark, *Vigilant* was 4 minutes, 45 seconds ahead. At the second mark, with an increasing breeze, *Vigilant* gained until she was 10 mintues ahead.

The boats gybed around the second mark and headed for home, again on a reach, this time in rather heavy weather, which wetted both boats' decks and crews. *Vigilant* gained again, and so it was her race all the way, with a victory by more than 10 minutes at the end.

On October 11 a race was begun, the wind died and the crews sat out the time limit and then were towed home. The third race was finally sailed on October 13.

It was Friday the thirteenth and the race seemed to begin under conditions to justify the fears of the most superstitious sailor. First came gale warnings from the weather men. Second, one of the throat halyard blocks of the *Vigilant* gave way when a strap parted, and the mainsail had to be lowered in order to repair it. While it was down the captain

Vigilant

smelled the wind and took a reef in his sail. The British captain, watching closely, did the same.

The race was set to begin at 11:25. Lord Dunraven had held that this was the starting time and it made no difference which vessel was in position or if neither was, the starting time should still be observed. At 11:25 in the morning the *Valkyrie II* was 3 miles behind the starting line, while *Vigilant* was very nearly in position. Had the starting gun sounded on schedule *Vigilant* would probably have gained a great advantage, however *Vigilant* discovered that her bronze centerboard was jammed and could not be lowered. Many minutes passed as the British finished reefing sail and came up, and the sailors on *Vigilant* pried at the centerboard. Finally, the centerboard was released and the starting gun fired at 12:27.

The course was again the 15 miles to windward and return. As the boats moved forward, *Vigilant* had the windward berth and it appeared that she would be able to blanket her opponent. But the British captain suddenly luffed, swung *Valkyrie II* into the wind, and moved around to the far side of the *Vigilant*. It was a stroke of superior seamanship.

Valkyrie II sailed better into the wind this day than *Vigilant,* staying closer into the wind and moving as fast. It was blowing hard, and both boats were smothered by spray, lying over in the gusts, with the crews hanging out over the windward rails to balance, every man as wet as a herring.

At the outer mark *Valkyrie II* was ahead by 600 yards, and since she was the faster boat in running before the wind, it seemed certain that she would win this race. She was almost 3 minutes ahead at the halfway point.

Friday the thirteenth descended on the Englishmen again. The crew hoisted *Valkyrie II's* spinnaker, sending it up loose, It caught on the bitts on the way up and was torn slightly. Then, the sail was caught in one of the fierce squalls which punctured the race and ripped to pieces in a few moments. Another spinnaker was hoisted, but it blew out too, and then the third and last bowsprit spinnaker was sent up, a much smaller sail, which at least held until the end of the race. The other sails were left alone, the main with its reef and the small topsail above it.

On the *Vigilant,* when the halfway mark was rounded and the crew saw that they were behind the *Valkyrie II,* every man knew that only desperate measures could win the race for the defender that day.

Vigilant's spinnaker went up and ballooned out without breaking. Then, however, the jib topsail halyard fouled and a man was sent up to the topmast head and then down the topmast stay to clear the sail. More sail was needed, that much was apparent. The way to get it was to take the reef out of the mainsail, but the normal way to do that was to spill the wind out of the sail and hoist it. This was inconceivable under the circumstances: it would have meant the loss of the race without doubt.

There was another way and this was followed.

No one had ever seen it done before under half-gale conditions, but there was no real alternative. A man was sent along the main boom, wearing a lifeline suspended from the masthead. He cut the reef knots as he moved along the boom. Meanwhile, another man was at the topmasthead, lashing the working topsail, clearing the topsail halyard and sending it down to the deck, while still another man at the gaff end was doing the same with the topsail sheet, keeping the working topsail in place. In this way, the mainsail could be shaken out and raised up when the reefs were cut and this was done while all the rest of the crew were pulling on the throat-and-peak halyards, hoisting that heavy mainsail as high as it would go, straining against the awful pressure of the wind.

When this was done, and the working topsail was still kept aloft, now overlapping the mainsail, a small jackyard topsail was sent up and sheeted home, the working topsail, too large for the mainsail extended, was brought down.

At every moment the strain on the mast was increased as this maneuver was carried out, and at the very end, as the mainsail was sweated up to its hightest point against the pressure of the wind, anything could have happened. If halyards or blocks gave way the *Vigilant* would have lost her keel and most of her way, and the race would have been lost irretrievably. Or a stay might have parted, a man might have been flung into the sea, and the maneuver failed. Worst of all, the mast might have broken under the strain, smashing up the deck, and crushing men, pushing others overboard, even dragging sails and rigging asea like an anchor and capsize the yacht.

Nothing like this maneuver had ever been seen in a yacht race. The result was the *Vigilant* caught up with *Valkyrie II,* her mast and rigging straining every moment. She passed the challenger, and kept moving away, all her canvas set and flying, at the finish leading by 2 minutes and 13 seconds, and after time allowances were made, winning the race by 40 seconds.

Once again, The Cup was saved, but this time by the most narrow margin, and really only by the most dauntless seamanship, against what may well have been a superior vessel. It certainly seemed that way, because the next year *Vigilant* went abroad to English waters to race, and there found her major opponent to be the *Valkyrie II's* sister ship, the Prince of Wales's *Britannia.* In 17 meetings, the *Britannia* won 12 to *Vigilant's* 5 races.

The only way to truly settle the matter would be for *Vigilant* and *Valkyrie II* to meet again. *Valkyrie II* spent the winter of 1893-4 in America, and then sailed home for the summer racing, so it seemed that they might meet. But in the first race of the 1894 season *Valkyrie II* was rammed amidships by the *Satanita* on the Clyde, and she sank within a few moments. So although The Cup races were decided fairly enough, the question about the two yachts was never settled and never could be.

9

Lord Dunraven Is Annoyed

Lord Dunraven had come closer than any other Englishman to winning back the 100 guinea cup that had been taken from England's shores by the yacht *America,* and with victory in such plain view it was natural that he would challenge again for the cup.

Not many days passed after the unfortunate sinking of the *Valkyrie II* before his lordship closeted himself again with Designer George Watson, planning a *Valkyrie III* which would challenge in the year 1895. The challenge was issued in good time and accepted, largely on the terms of the previous one.

Valkyrie III was very much a racing machine, the first that the British produced in this struggle to win the cup. The American underwater design of deep keel and broad beam was copied, on the theory that these craft sailed better in American waters. Three thousand feet more of sail surface were added in the design. All the Americans were told was that a cutter (one-masted boat) of 89 foot length would be coming to race the following year.

This news indicated that the New York Yacht Club must build a new boat for defense, because it was questionable whether or not *Vigilant* could hold her own against a boat 4 feet longer. It was obvious that the new British challenger would carrry far more sail.

A new syndicate was formed in New York to back the building of a boat. C. Oliver Iselin headed the group and brought in William K. Vanderbilt and E. D. Morgan. They gave the contract to Nathaniel Herreshoff once again. This time, while the British builder was turning to the American design, the American builder turned to the deep, narrow lines that had always characterized the challengers before. When finished the new yacht, called *Defender,* was slightly smaller than *Valkyrie III* (88 feet long at the waterline) and carried about a thousand feet less of canvas.

In 1895 as in other years, American yachtsmen took their racing too

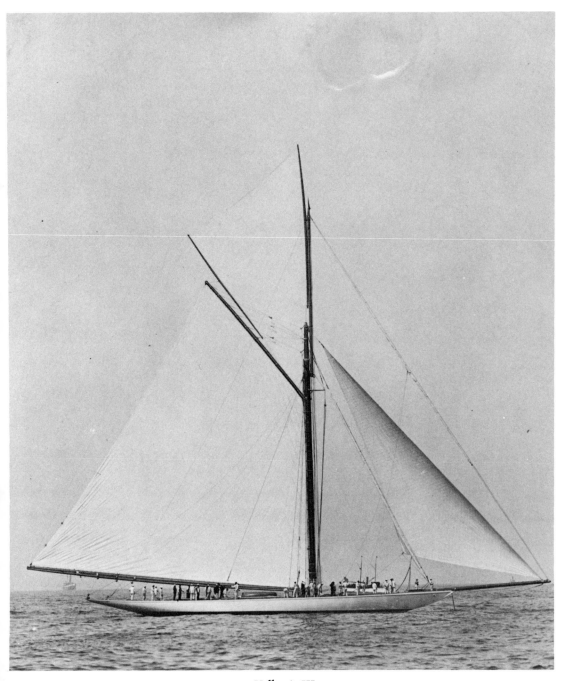

Valkyrie III

Defender

seriously to be very good sportsmen, and what began as ordinary trials between the new *Defender* and the old *Vigilant* ended up in a duel of fouls, charges, and squabbling, which marred The America's Cup challenge even before the challenger was brought into it.

Valkyrie III arrived on August 19, and went into drydock for a few days, then began tuning up for the races, which were to begin on September 7.

The course for the first race was 15 miles to windward and return, starting from the Scotland lightship outside New York Harbor. This year so much interest in the cup races had been aroused that the course was lined by excursion steamers and small boats, which from the beginning threatened to be a problem in the racing. This year, for the first time, the number of pleasure boats really interfered with the starting of the race, because the yachts could not maneuver freely behind the starting line.

Finally they did get away in a light breeze around noon. *Defender* got away first, and pointed well into the wind, but it was soon apparent that *Valkyrie III* was the faster boat, and she passed the *Defender*. At that point the American captain turned onto the other tack and so the boats sailed away from each other into the wind, then tacked and headed back toward the center line, making a diamond pattern in theory. As they approached each other it could be seen that while *Valkyrie III* sailed faster, *Defender* sailed more closely into the wind, and this levelled out the advantages. *Defender* managed just barely to slip across the bows of *Valkyrie III* as they passed on their opposite tacks. At the halfway mark *Defender* had a good lead, and then coming home, the new American, or old British style of the *Defender* was better suited for sailing with the wind than the new British, or old American style of *Valkyrie III*. The reason was that the weather was most unusual, and the sea was rough with a heavy swell, conditions quite common in English waters and very uncommon in New York waters. In normal American weather *Valkyrie's* broad, flat hull would have been much faster.

The Americans won the first race, then, by nearly 9 minutes.

When the second race began on September 10, *Valkyrie III* started to windward of the *Defender*, sailing away from the line and then gybed around to get her running start. *Defender* did the same, and the two boats sailed almost parallel courses. Then an excursion steamer, the *Yorktown*, came across the path of the yachts, endangering both of them. *Valkyrie* passed on the windward side of the steamer and *Defender* passed on the leeward side. Then, because he was in a bad position for the start, the captain of *Defender* moved closer into the wind. The *Valkyrie* changed course to try to blanket the *Defender* from the wind and hinder her start, and as *Valkyrie III* changed, her boom came across sharply, striking the topmast stay in the bow of the other boat and breaking off. *Defender's* topmast cracked, and Oliver Iselin immediately hoisted a protest flag—indicating that he believed the foul had been the fault of *Valkyrie III* and not an accident.

The most sportsmanlike procedure would have called for Lord Dunraven to find out immediately how much damage had been done to his opponent. He did not, for this was a cup race, and sailed on. *Defender* sailed on, too, although she did not sail very well on the starboard tack, because of the sagging topmast. *Valkyrie III* moved into the lead and stayed there. On the reach home along the last leg of the triangular course of this second race, *Defender* moved up but she could not catch *Valkyrie III,* and came across the line 2 minutes and 18 seconds after her, losing by 47 seconds when her time allowance was granted.

Then began a correspondence between the race committee, the head of the American syndicate and Lord Dunraven. Dunraven took the position that the foul was an accident. He would have been happy enough to sail the race over and that is what Iselin suggested, yet by making an official protest, Iselin had levied the claim that the *Valkyrie III* had committed the foul, and the committee agreed, hence the race was automatically given to the American *Defender* on a foul. Dunraven then retired in hauteur and refused to sail the race over, although Iselin again suggested it.

Dunraven was angry. He protested to the committee about the crowding by the excursion fleet. At one point he indicated that he would not sail another race unless the committee would eliminate the steamers whose wash splashed into the *Valkyrie III* constantly, and which were forever crossing her bows during the races.

The third race was held on September 12. *Defender* had a new topmast, and on it she had a large club topsail set. *Valkyrie III* had not set her topsail at all. This seemed odd to the spectators.

What they did not know was that Dunraven was truly angry about the interference of the steamers in addition to all else. After the first race he had complained. He had also complained after that race because someone had indicated to him that *Defender* had shifted her ballast between the pre-race inspection and the race. When the committee had investigated that second charge no appreciable difference in waterline could be seen, but Dunraven's crew was still not totally convinced. Then, after the second race in which the accident had obviously been caused by the discourteous steamer, Dunraven had protested mightily. The committee had not responded satisfactorily to his protests. He had suggested that the steamers be cleared from the area, or that the race be held in some unpublicized spot, or that the committee at least take responsibility to try to determine whether or not the steamers were interfering with the race, and that if either racer was bothered, the committee would declare the race invalid and have it sailed over.

The race committee did not respond to this last request. Then, on the night before that third race, Dunraven said that if the committee would not do this, he would sail across the line to give *Defender* a start, but then he would retire from the race.

Apparently this letter was delayed in transit. At least the committee received it only on the morning of the race, and then did not consider it seriously or considered it so stiff-neckedly that nothing was done.

That was the explanation of the slackness of *Valkyrie's* rig as the race began. *Defender* crossed the line. She was followed closely by *Valkyrie III* then, as soon as the line was cleared, *Valkyrie III* luffed up into the wind, hauled down her racing flag and hauled up the burgee of the New York Yacht Club. She recrossed the line and returned to her mooring place. Lord Dunraven had retired from the race.

Defender sailed around, and returned, thus completing the course and officially winning the race and the series. But it was truly no contest.

It was an unpleasant end to the series. The air became more unpleasant later. The American newsapers attacked Lord Dunraven's sportsmanship. On his return to England, Dunraven renewed the claim that the crew of *Defender* had tampered with her ballast as early as the first race, and he based it on observation of something being carried all night long from the *Defender's* tender to the yacht before the race.

A special committee of the New York Yacht Club was appointed to look into the charges, a committee made up of men of such known integrity as J. Pierpont Morgan, William C. Whitney, and the Hon. E. J. Phelps, who had been American minister to England (all these men were well and favorably known in England). Dunraven said there could be no real investigation. It was too late. Yet he did come to America to make his statements before the committee.

It was discovered in the investigation that Dunraven had indeed seen ballast going aboard the *Defender*. The race committee had allowed *Defender* to replace bulkheads and other fittings with ballast, because *Valkyrie III* did not come over with bulkheads, water tanks, and such fittings. What Dunraven had seen that night was the taking on of 63 pigs of lead, which exactly equalized three tons of fittings taken out of the *Defender* earlier that day. Then, some of the pigs did not fit and could not be stowed, so it took a night of work to make the yacht fit for the race.

When the facts came to light, Dunraven was expected to apologize for the charges. He did not. Then *his* resignation as an honorary member of the New York Yacht Club was asked. He did not respond, so he was expelled from the club.

At about this same time a challenge was received from another English yacht club, but so heated did the argument become, and with so much feeling engendered on both sides, that the challenge was withdrawn.

Dunraven's position was not particulary admired in England, but the general feeling there was that The America's Cup races had become a most unpleasant matter at best, and that it would be more sensible and wiser to forget about them for a number of years.

10

The Lipton Challenges

In spite of any rights or wrongs in the Dunraven case, the members of the New York Yacht Club were not very happy with the outcome of The America's Cup defenses in recent times, and did not really expect anything to happen in the near future which would remove the tarnish that had seemed to gather on the cup. They were delighted when in the summer of 1898 there came a cable from the Royal Ulster Yacht Club of Belfast, Ireland, announcing that Sir Thomas Lipton, the tea merchant, was interested in making a challenge on behalf of his club and would send a committee to discuss the matter.

When the committee of three members arrived in New York it took very little time to arrange the conditions for the races, and both sides announced themselves as very well satisfied with the conditions.

The surprise of the Americans was matched in England. Sir Thomas was not one of the old line British aristocrats, but one of the new baronets who had earned his honors in trade. Some of the more conservative British yachtsmen grumbled quietly that this was a fitting challenger for the annoying Americans. Others wondered what Sir Thomas could possibly know about yachts, since his experience, aside from tea, was in traveling about on the world's seas in the *Erin,* a steam yacht he had bought a number of years before.

But the fact was that Sir Thomas knew a great deal about yachting, because he had been following the sport and The America's Cup matches in particular, for a number of years. Besides, there had been a considerable change in the conditions of The America's Cup races in the last few years. Earlier, the races had been run by yachtsmen. But the *Thistle* had been a syndicate boat, and Dunraven was more the rich man than the yachtsman. So was Sir Thomas Lipton, although he was a rich man who aspired to become a sportsman.

When the committee from the yacht club came to New York, it was accompanied by William Fife, a naval architect who had been given the commission to design a racing machine for The America's Cup. That was what it was to be, a racing machine. The development had been in that direction in the last few defenses of the cup, and *Valkyrie III* had been a knocked-down yacht, quite incapable of taking serious cruising roughness, while *Defender* was so unseaworthy that her backers worried during the races lest she knock her mast through the bottom before the season ended.

Lipton's first racing yacht, for that is what she was, turned out to be very much like *Defender* in construction. She was the largest challenger yet built, almost 90 feet long at the waterline, carrying 13,492 square feet of sail. She was built flat and broad, to take advantage of the prevailing American water conditions. She was called the *Shamrock*.

This year the American syndicate to build the defending boat was headed by J. Pierpont Morgan, the banker. Oliver Iselin was again given the responsibility as manager of the syndicate, however. Herreshoff was chosen to build the boat, which was very similar in appearance to the *Shamrock*. She was called *Columbia*, and was a little longer overall than *Shamrock*, although exactly the same length at the waterline, a little narrower in the beam, and she carried a few hundred feet less of sail.

Earlier yachts had sailed across the Atlantic to compete for The America's Cup. The *Shamrock* was towed most of the way across behind the *Erin*, but no one seemed to mind.

All during the yachting season *Columbia* had raced against other sloops and particularly against *Defender*, but it was still the practice to have a trial race for the position of official defender of the cup, and early in September *Columbia* defeated *Defender* twice to secure the honor.

This year everyone connected with the race was conscious of the troublesome spectators, and a fleet of federal revenue cutters and torpedo boats was brought out to keep them away from the race course. The first race was supposed to be held on October 3, but the boats were becalmed during the race and it was called off. Then came 2 solid weeks of calm and fog, and the race was not held until October 16.

Columbia won the first race, 10 minutes and 11 seconds ahead of *Shamrock*. In the second race *Shamrock's* club topsail collapsed 25 minutes after the start, when the boats were neck and neck. By the time the hanging sail was cleared away she was out of the race and accepted a tow home. Under the conditions of the race, *Columbia* could not turn about and call it off even if her captain wanted to. She sailed the course and was credited with victory.

The third race was again won by *Columbia* by 6 minutes, and that was that. Sir Thomas Lipton did not complain about anything, and so grateful

Shamrock

Columbia in drydock, 1899

Columbia

Columbia's Corinthians

was the New York Yacht Club that Commodore Pierpont Morgan proposed him for honorary membership and he was quickly accepted. He left America amid applause and with talk of another challenge.

The challenge did not come for a year, because Sir Thomas wanted to give any other challenger an opportunity if he wished to enter the contest. None did, so on October 2, 1900, he challenged again for the following summer. George Watson built him a new boat, a 90 foot cutter which was named *Shamrock II.* She was 10 feet longer overall than the old *Shamrock,* and she carried 14,027 feet of sail.

In America a new syndicate was formed, and Herreshoff again received the order for the boat. This defender was to be called *Constitution.* She was as large as the *Shamrock II,* and carried 200 square feet more of sail than the British boat.

That summer in America there was a great contest to see which yacht would defend for The Cup in 1901. The New York Yacht Club syndicate expected, of course, that its boat would be selected. E. D. Morgan of the club bought out Oliver Iselin's share of *Columbia* and entered that old defender in the proceedings. From Boston there came word that Thomas W. Lawson, a wealthy stockbroker, would build a defender too, and he did, a big sloop called the *Independence.*

The club informed Lawson, as a matter of course, that he would either have to join the New York Yacht Club or put his boat in the name of a member if he wanted to join the cup trials. Lawson refused to do either.

During the summer *Columbia* and *Constitution* raced several times, and *Columbia* kept winning. Late in the summer *Independence* came down from Boston, and turned out to be a radically designed racing scow, with huge sail spread, unwieldy in anything but the most favorable weather. The Newport Yacht Racing Association arranged some races, and in these *Independence* finished last 6 times, which put an end to her bid.

Constitution and *Columbia* met 22 times that summer—each winning 9 of the finished races. After much consideration of form and seamanship The Cup Committee chose *Columbia* again to defend, much to the disappointment of August Belmont and other members of the syndicate which had backed the new boat.

Shamrock II encountered some difficulties in her trials on the other side of the Atlantic. One day when the Prince of Wales (who would be Edward VII) was aboard, the yacht lost her mast off Cowes. She was heeling over in a puff of wind when the mast crumpled and went over the side, impaling itself in the mud and anchoring her firmly. No one was hurt. The Prince calmly lit a cigar and watched the salvage operations. They were considerable. The mast could not be released, so the captain had to send into Cowes for torches to cut the mast away.

The accident brought about a request from Sir Thomas that the races be delayed for a month, and this delay was granted. There was a warning in the incident for all who would see: The Cup racers had reached a limit on sail capacity. In their eagerness to compete, the designers were building nothing but speed platforms, not yachts that could be relied upon for safety or seaworthiness. The racing yacht was getting out of hand.

In this race series, many on both sides of the ocean believed *Shamrock II* was going to win. *Columbia* won the first race by 35 seconds, and by 1 minute, 20 seconds corrected time; she won the second race, and then she won the third race by 41 seconds, although *Shamrock* actually crossed the finish line 2 seconds ahead of the American boat. Still, these were the closest races ever held for The Cup, and they aroused more enthusiasm among the public than had ever been seen.

After the incident of *Shamrock II's* 1901 dismasting in public view, one might have expected that the challengers and defenders would have decided to do away with the racing scow, those huge, useless platforms for sail, that had taken command of The Cup races. But no, Sir Thomas asked for another race in 1903 and built *Shamrock III*. True, she was not as unwieldy as *Shamrock II*, but she was almost 90 feet long, 134 feet long on deck, and she carried 14,154 square feet of sail. The Americans again formed a syndicate, this time involving Cornelius Vanderbilt of the railroad family, William Rockefeller of the oil family, Elbert H. Gary of United States Steel, and half a dozen other millionaires. This year no expense at all was spared in building the boat the syndicate hoped would defend the cup. The new boat, *Reliance*, cost $175,000. She was flat, with a shallow body, long ends, and a deep fin keel, a skimming dish with a deep weight to hold her down. The greatest accomplishment of the Herreshoff yard in building her was to put 16,160 square feet of canvas on her. She was the most extreme cup yacht yet designed.

Shamrock III again showed what was wrong with the racing yachts. In a race with old *Shamrock I* in Weymouth Bay on the south coast of England, *Shamrock III* was dismasted by a puff of wind. The whole rigging collapsed and went over the side. Several crew members were injured and one man was swept overboard and drowned. Sir Thomas was very much upset by the accident.

In America this year *Columbia* was again brought forth to try out against the new boat, and so was *Constitution*, the old syndicate boat that had never proved good enough for the task. On July 27 the three boats raced for the honor of defending The Cup and *Reliance* won, beating *Columbia* by only 46 seconds, and *Constitution* by 2 minutes and 29

Shamrock II

Shamrock III

Reliance

seconds.

The races were held late in August. *Shamrock III* brought *Shamrock I* across the Atlantic with her to help "tune up." *Reliance* won the first race by 7 minutes, due largely to bad sail handling by the *Shamrock III's* crew. *Reliance* won the second race by a corrected time of a minute and 19 seconds. Then there was a 9 day delay because there was not enough wind, and a one day delay because there was too much wind. These yachts had grown so large and carried so much sail that in heavy weather they might very easily be dismasted.

The finish of the series of 1903 was almost foolish. Day after day the weather turned bad, and on September 3 a race was held, even though the weather was foggy to start. The racers were so weary of delays that they were willing to accept any conditions. In the fog no one could see what was happening, until *Reliance* finally appeared out of the murk and crossed the finish line. *Shamrock III* had gotten lost and was discovered some time later well northeast of the lightship, which she had never found in the bad weather.

And so that was the end of the series. More, it was the end of America's Cup racing for a long time. One problem, the greatest possible problem, had made itself quite clear this year. Under the challenge terms, all that the American defenders needed to do to retain possession of the cup was to outbuild the challengers. This had been done in 1903 with *Reliance,* which carried three times as much sail as the *America* had carried. Was it a yacht? It hardly seemed to be a yacht when its crew feared that in winds of more than 12 or 14 knots she might be dismasted, and when the racing committee had to put into effect a rule that the races could be called off in weather that older yachtsmen would have termed "fresh." The Americans were not alone; the *Shamrocks* were the same type of boats. The system was at fault; the competition was based on the wrong premises, putting money and size at premium, and in a sense, distorting the entire concept of The America's Cup races in the beginning.

After 1903 no one wanted to challenge again, for it would have meant a bigger boat with bigger mast and bigger sails and the Americans would build something bigger and faster in all probability.

For several years there were no challenges at all, then in 1907 Sir Thomas issued a conditional challenge. The condition was that the races be held under a new rule, which would take into account the displacement of the racing craft as well as the length and sail area. Actually by this time both in America and in Europe such rules had been brought into force by yachting officials to control yacht racing. Still, when Sir Thomas brought the matter up, some conservatives in the New York Yacht Club held out for races under the old rules set down by George Schuyler. The truth was that many New York Yacht Club members were tired of seeing Sir Thomas as the perennial contender and wanted a new challenger.

Yet none showed up. In 1912 after some preliminary negotiating Sir Thomas challenged with a 75 foot boat. She was called *Shamrock IV*. She carried 10,459 feet of canvas, a considerable amount for her size. Three American boats were built to defend the cup—the *Resolute,* built by a yacht club syndicate, the *Vanitie,* built for Alexander S. Cochran, and a boat named *Defiance,* which was built for a second New York Yacht Club syndicate by a Boston naval architect.

The races were scheduled for the summer for the 1914. *Shamrock IV* was on her way across the Atlantic and had actually reached Bermuda, when the outbreak of World War I came in August. She came on to New York, but Sir Thomas requested that the races be postponed indefinitely. When his country was at war it was no time for him to be playing games.

11

The Match of 1920

Two years after the end of World War I it was agreed that the race postponed for so long could be held and Sir Thomas Lipton's challenger, *Shamrock IV* began to make ready, while two American yachts contested for the right to defend the cup in behalf of the New York Yacht Club.

This year for the first time in a half century, there was no special building of yachts for the cup races. One might say that yacht design simply stood still, as far as cup boats were concerned, while the nations of the world turned to more important matters.

Resolute and *Vanitie* sailed 11 races in the spring and summer of 1920. In the first race *Resolute* lost her mast in a squall. In the second, she broke the jaws on her gaff, but won the race anyhow. *Vanitie* won the third race, and then the yachts began trading victories. In one contest *Vanitie* picked up a lobster pot buoy on her keel, which caused her to lose. In the end, although the yachts were very evenly matched and sailed by a good crew, the committee picked *Resolute* because she won 7 of the 11 races.

The challenger was busy, too, that spring. Sir Thomas had his old *Shamrock I* brought to the United States to race with the new boat, and a number of informal races were held to tune up the *Shamrock IV* to her best sailing ability.

The America's Cup races of 1920 were marked by one important change over the past: both racers were to be sailed by amateur captains, which showed how much racing had changed in a half a century from a sport of the very rich, in which they watched, largely, but did not participate, into an active sport. Captain of the challenger was to be William P. Burton, one of the best-known amateurs in England. Captain of the defender was Charles Francis Adams of Boston, one of America's most enthusiastic skippers.

The races were set to begin on July 15. Once again the course was laid out off Sandy Hook, with the starting line for the first race placed near the Ambrose light vessel. *Resolute* got away to a better start and was sailed better in the first race, at least to the halfway point where she was half a mile ahead. Then, watchers saw *Resolute's* mainsail sag halfway down the mast. Her wire throat halyards had broken at the hoisting winch below deck, and the goose-neck of the gaff had jumped loose, which made it impossible to reset the mainsail. So, *Resolute* was out of the race, and the challengers won the first round.

It was hard to tell which boat would win the series. Both were fast. *Resolute* seemed to sail closer to windward; *Shamrock IV* traveled faster through the water, but *Shamrock's* flat nose did not ride in the water as well as *Resolute's* slimmer bow. Captain Burton had made a serious mistake in tacking at one point in the first half of the race and had lost valuable time, but this could be attributed more to lack of knowledge of local waters than to bad seamanship. So it was still anyone's series.

The second race was not sailed until July 20 because the weather was so fluky until that day. Even on July 20 the breeze was very light. In the past this had almost always worked to the benefit of the defender, because boats were built to work well in light wind.

The race began at 12:15 in a wind that was clocked at just 4 knots. It was to be a three-leg race around the triangular course. *Shamrock IV* got away to a good start, but as she crossed the line and let out her balloon jib, the sail fouled about 25 feet above the bowsprit and hung limp, much like a deflated balloon. *Resolute* had no such trouble; her ballooner went up quickly and filled out.

Shamrock's crew tore the balloon sail in getting it in and it was useless, so *Resolute* had a definite edge. *Shamrock* sent up a spinnaker to starboard, but it would not fill in the light wind. Something had to be done and Captain Burton improvised. He sent a sailor aloft to put a strap around the mast about two thirds of the way up to the lower masthead, and a block was fixed to this, and then a small light sail was set from the bowsprit to this block. It was unusual, but it worked, and *Shamrock* began pulling after *Resolute,* which had drawn about a quarter of a mile ahead.

Shamrock IV, with these sails, was able to sail more closely into the wind than *Resolute,* flying the balloon. She passed *Resolute,* then gained about a half mile on her, while *Resolute* sat nearly becalmed.

On the second leg the sails and the wind favored *Shamrock,* and she drew even further ahead, rounding the marker nine minutes ahead of *Resolute.* Burton had to win by 7 minutes and 39 seconds, because that was the time allowance he had been forced to give, owing to the greater size and displacement of the *Shamrock.* He did win, by 2 minutes and 26

Launch of *Shamrock IV*

Shamrock IV

Resolute

Crew of the *Resolute*

seconds, corrected time, which meant the *Shamrock IV* came over the line some 10 minutes ahead of *Resolute.*

Now the British challenger had won two races and needed only one more of the next three, to win the cup. Here chances were brighter than those of any previous challenger.

The race of July 21 was the closest America's Cup race ever held. Both boats were sailed with great skill, and they covered the course in exactly the same time. This meant, however, that since both came home in 4 hours, 3 minutes, and 6 seconds, that *Resolute* won the race because of her time allowance. So the series stood two to one in favor of the challenger.

In the fourth race, after a good start, Captain Burton split his tack and ran into a soft spot where the wind seemed to die down. This cost him dearly in the first minutes of the race, and *Resolute* led by more than 2 minutes at the end of the first leg. On the second leg *Shamrock IV* moved up, but was able to only gain back 43 seconds of lost time, because the defenders handled their sails with unusual skill. On the last leg the *Resolute* drew ahead, showing superior qualities in reaching in the strong wind, and there was never a doubt about the outcome. *Resolute* crossed the finish 3 minutes and 18 seconds ahead of the challenger.

Now the series was all even. This final race would decide the possession of the coveted Cup.

This was by far the most exciting series of races that had ever been held, and, in the three days that elapsed before the final race, huge crowds of people jammed the excursion steamers that came to watch the yachts, even though the tourists were disappointed day after day. The weather was too *heavy.*

The start came at 2:15 in the afternoon of July 27, in a very light and unsatisfactory wind. From the beginning everything seemed to go wrong for the challenger. She hit a soft spot on the first leg, and *Resolute* rounded the mark 4 minutes ahead. She found another soft spot on the way home (this was a windward-and-return race) and she bogged down so that with the time allowance, *Resolute* won the race by the margin of 19 minutes and 45 seconds.

So the cup was safe again, although for several days it had seemed very much in danger.

12

The J-Boats

Nearly ten years passed before another challenge came from anywhere to race the New York Yacht Club's chosen defender of The America's Cup. One reason for the delay was that the building of huge racing platforms had become far too expensive in a modern world, and there had been much criticism of The America's Cup racers after the races of 1920 because they could not stand what to other yachts would be a very fair breeze. A strong wind would tear the masts out of any Cup boat.

In the ten years after 1920, however, there were important changes in naval architecture and in yachting practice. An international agreement was reached on the construction and rating of various yachts. Several classes were established. Class J, for example, meant basically a boat of 76 feet; Class K meant a boat of 65 feet. Yet the rules allowed for variations which the designer could use as he wished. For instance, a J-boat could have a waterline as long as 87 feet, as long as it met other specifications which would put it on an equal par with boats that might have shorter waterlines, but stronger capabilities in other directions.

Another great change was discovery of aerodynamic principles which proved that a tall narrow sail was far sounder than the short broad ones that racing boats had been using for a century.

With the use of these new discoveries, designers could build boats that carried perhaps 7500 feet of sail, yet sailed as fast as the old boats that carried 16,000 feet. The new rig was called the Bermudian rig. It consisted of an immensely tall mast carrying a single triangular mainsail. There were no more topsails to be run on a boom above the gaff of the mainsail. The main boom also was brought in; it no longer projected so far over the stern that it would foul the stays of a boat close behind, as had happened with Lord Dunraven's *Valkyrie III.*

Now, two basic changes were possible in The America's Cup races. The challenger and the defender would both be real sailing yachts, and not racing boats, and they would be as evenly matched as a formula could

80

W. Starling Burgess

Enterprise

Harold S. Vanderbilt, W. Starling Burgess, and others

make them. Second, they could really race, without the complicated formulation of time allowances, in which it was possible for two boats to set out from a mark at the same time, with one boat winning handily in the "race" yet have the judges announce that the loser was really the winner because of handicap. The time allowance was fair enough, but it did not make for very exciting sport.

Sir Thomas Lipton challenged again, for races to be run in 1930, and he agreed to build a J-boat. There would be more races this year; the winner would be the boat that took the best four of a possible seven races. And, finally, the course was to be changed. New York Harbor was too filled with commercial traffic and flotsam and jetsam to make it sensible to race there any longer. The races would be moved this year to a course in the open water off Newport, Rhode Island, where the breezes blew fresher and more steadily.

This year, in spite of the Wall Street Crash of 1929 and the depression that began in 1930, four potential defenders were built. Had the races not been arranged so early in 1929 perhaps there would not have been so many prospects, but in the spring and summer of that year the United States seemed to be bathed in endless prosperity and any number of wealthy men were eager to contribute to the defense of The Cup. One New York Yacht Club syndicate, headed by Winthrop Aldrich, had a boat built by W. Starling Burgess, son of the old designer of Cup defenders. She was called the *Enterprise.*

Another syndicate, headed by Junius S. Morgan, grandson of J. Pierpont, built a boat called *Weetamoe,* designed by Clinton H. Crane. John S. Lawrence of Boston formed a syndicate which built a boat called *Yankee,* designed by Frank Paine, of the family of old General Paine. A fourth syndicate, led by Landon K. Thorne, sought the Herreshoffs again to build *Whirlwind.*

When the boats were built, all turned out to be keelboats, except that several of them also had small centerboards to help balance the yachts. The rule held that sail area had to be within 7550 and 7583 square feet. *Enterprise,* the smallest of the yachts, carried the most sail: 7583 feet. *Yankee* and *Whirlwind* both carried the minimum 7550, and *Weetamoe* spread 7560 square feet.

The mainsails were all alike—tall and triangular. Forward of the mast, the boats were more like the older cup boats, carrying triple rigs: forestaysail, jig, and jib topsail. There were several sizes of jib topsails, to be used in various strengths of wind. Genoa jibs were sometimes used, but they were valuable to these boats only in very light wind, and spinnakers were very much like the old spinnakers of the sailing platforms.

All during the summer the American yachts raced among themselves. *Resolute* and *Vanitie* were rerigged so they could race with the other four boats, and the competition was keen in every race. *Yankee* and *Whirlwind*, the largest yachts of the four hopeful defenders, were at their best when there was plenty of wind. *Enterprise* and *Weetamoe* sailed best in light breezes, but before the end of the season *Enterprise* and *Weetamoe* won most of the races.

At the end of August the official trial races were held on the new courses, which began and ended at a buoy 9 miles southeast of Brenton's Reef lightship, not far from Newport. The four J-boats were raced in pairs. Thirteen races were finished over 30 mile courses, and of these *Weetamoe* had won five and *Enterprise* had won four. *Weetamoe* was, then, the favorite to defend The Cup.

Harold S. Vanderbuilt, the captain of *Enterprise,* was the busiest man in the summer fleet. There was no end to the rigging changes he made in his boat. Although *Weetamoe* was favored, when the New York Yacht Club went on its annual cruise in August, the decision still had not been made, and during the racing on the cruise, Vanderbilt's experiments paid off and he won three races, *Weetamoe* won three, and *Yankee* captured one race.

The final trials for the defense of The Cup were held on The Cup course on August 20, with Sir Thomas and the men who would supervise *Shamrock V's* challenge watching aboard the steam yacht *Erin.*

Enterprise won the first race in a light breeze, ranging from 6 to 12 miles an hour. The next day the wind was racing at 25 miles from the northeast, and *Enterprise* won again, beating *Weetamoe* by 3 minutes. *Yankee,* that day, set a new course record of 2 hours, 47 minutes, and 59 seconds, in racing with *Whirlwind,* but later the committee selected *Enterprise* as the cup defender, on the basis of her overall record for the season.

This year, in order to eliminate any interference from the spectator fleet, the United States Coast Guard and the U. S. Navy brought in cutters and destroyers and small craft to control the racing area. Two lines of ships were laid out, flanking the race course but far enough away so as not to trouble the racers.

The 1930 Cup races were far less exciting than the trials. The weather, for one thing, was not what it might have been, and the first race was described by one reporter as the dullest race sailed in American waters all year. Captain Vanderbilt took *Enterprise* out in front at the start and led all the way, finishing 2 minutes and 52 seconds ahead. *Enterprise* won the second race by more than 9 minutes. *Shamrock V* made a better start in the third race, and managed to blanket *Enterprise* for a few minutes, but

Shamrock V

Rainbow

Vanderbilt tacked away from his opponent and cleared his wind and began to edge ahead. Then *Shamrock's* main halyard gave away, and the mainsail sagged. *Enterprise* sailed around the course, but the race was over, *Shamrock* having to default. The fourth race was sailed in the best wind of the series at 14 knots over a triangular course. The crew of *Enterprise* noticed a change in the wind before the *Shamrock* and got off to a fine start, increasing the lead until at the halfway mark the defender was 9 minutes and 10 seconds ahead. She loafed home, letting *Shamrock V* catch up a bit, and still won the race by 5 minutes and 44 seconds, to finish the series of 1930.

Sir Thomas Lipton said he would not challenge again. He was 82 years old that year, and having challenged for the cup 5 times in 30 years was convinced that he could not win. For all his challenges his rewards were a handful of cups given him and won in America, an invitation, when he was 82 years old, to join the Royal Yacht Squadron after many years of being ingnored because he was in trade, and a reputation as a sportsman that excelled even his reputation as a tea merchant. It was quite a collection.

Another J-boat challenge came within three years, now that the conditions of the race had been made so much more palatable to the English yachtsmen. T. O. M. Sopwith challenged in 1933 in behalf of the Royal Yacht Squadron.

It was impossible for the defending New York Yacht Club to use *Enterprise* again in The Cup races, because the rules governing J-boats had been changed. For one thing, there was much criticism of the original J-boats because they did not provide living accommodations for their crews, and were, as their critics said, simply racing shells.

Harold Vanderbilt led a syndicate this year which built *Rainbow*. Several of the older J-boats were reconditioned and changed enough to compete in the trials, and they were not to be laughed at. *Yankee* beat *Rainbow* 4 times in the first 2 months of racing in 1934 and *Weetamoe* was also a strong contender, although not nearly so strong as the other two. As the date for decision neared in summer, *Rainbow*, the new boat, was really very much second choice to *Yankee* and once again Harold Vanderbilt began experimenting.

There was a change in the rules this year, which allowed the British challengers to substitute another boat up to 60 days before the races, and this gave rise to an intense competition between Sopwith's *Endeavour*, and another British cutter named *Velsheda*. *Endeavour* won out. Then, just before she left for America her professional sailing crew struck for higher wages, and Sopwith fired them all, and replaced them with amateur sailors. In all, the *Endeavour* had only 9 professionals aboard when she came to try for the cup.

The struggle for the honor of defending the cup continued all summer as it had in 1930, in about the same fashion, with *Yankee* winning the races, and with Vanderbilt's *Rainbow* constantly cutting the time by which the other boat won. On the eve of the official trials, using a point for finishing and one for every yacht beaten, *Yankee* had 22 points and *Rainbow* had 16. Then *Rainbow* defeated *Yankee* in the cup trials, and they raced again. In this race *Yankee* broke a strut; had she not, it was learned later, and had she won, she would have been named cup defender for 1934.

In the next race *Rainbow* won, and in the final race, *Yankee* was ahead, then she split her Genoa jib and fell behind at the halfway point, then she gained back again and came to *Rainbow,* so that they finished overlapping, and *Rainbow* was declared the winner by one second.

The two boats were obviously well-matched and the trials had to end sometime. They ended that night. *Rainbow* was chosen to defend the America's Cup in 1934.

This year challenger and defender were very similar boats, as the following table shows:

	Waterline (feet)	Overall (feet)	Beam (feet)	Draft (feet)	Displacement (Long tons)	Sail Area (Square Feet)
Endeavour	83.3	129.7	22	14.9	143.1	7561
Rainbow	82	126.7	21	14.6	141.1	7572

Ten thousand spectators came out to watch on September 15 when the first race was scheduled. The breeze was light—too light—and died out altogether leaving the yachts stranded so they could not finish in the 5½ hour time limit.

Two days later the first race was sailed officially. *Endeavour* got off to a bad start, because a man was injured in a boatswain's chair when he tried to free the main halyard which had fouled on the spreaders. This brought about a 15 minute delay in the start, and even when the start was made *Endeavour* was not quite prepared, so *Rainbow* went into the lead. *Endeavour* sailed so well that she came up to within 18 seconds of *Rainbow* at the buoy. Then *Rainbow's* men were faster in setting the parachute spinnaker, but once their's was up, *Endeavour* sailed faster and passed *Rainbow,* sailed home ahead of her and won the race by 2 minutes and 9 seconds.

Endeavour won the second race, but only by 51 seconds.

Endeavour

In the third race, *Endeavour* seemed to have it won. She went out and passed the halfway mark 6 minutes and 39 seconds ahead of *Rainbow*. Then the wind dropped almost completely, and in trying to come home as quickly as possible *Endeavour* tacked quickly twice, in search of wind. She did not find it, and the tacking lost her headway so that in what was almost a flat calm *Rainbow* was able to slide home, and win by 3 minutes and 26 seconds. This race seemed lost at one point to *Rainbow*, and Captain Vanderbilt went below for a sandwich. By the time he came back up on deck, his boat was ahead of *Endeavour*, and she stayed there.

After this race, hoping to win another, Harold Vanderbilt secured the services of Frank Paine, designer of *Yankee* and sail trimming officer of that crew. Paine came along to Newport, bringing with him the best spinnaker from *Yankee*, and that night Vanderbilt also took on two more tons of ballast, hoping to help his boat.

The fourth race was over the triangle course. In the first leg of the race, *Rainbow* led, but as they came to the buoy and were to tack around it, *Endeavour* was so close to *Rainbow*, on the weather side, that *Rainbow* could not tack without fouling *Endeavour*. So *Endeavour* sat there and forced *Rainbow* to ride on several lengths, then *Endeavour* tacked inside the American boat, and gained the lead. The British crew was slow in getting Genoa jib set, however, and *Rainbow* then came up and began to pass to windward.

There was a rule that said if a boat was being overtaken and passed to windward, the captain could luff up into the wind, turning to prevent the other boat from passing, but only if his boat would strike the other foreward of the mast if the passing boat did not fall off. *Endeavour* turned to luff. *Rainbow* held her position. Rather than slice through the other boat, *Endeavour* turned away, and *Rainbow* took a lead she held all the rest of the way in.

The rules said that a protest flag must be raised immediately after the incident in protest, but *Endeavour* waited until she came home to fly her red flag. That night her captain did protest. The race committee stuck by the rules of the book which were almost never honored elsewhere, and said they would not consider the protest because the flag was flown too late. It was a technicality, and it caused a good deal of hard feeling. Later the committee said they had seen a foul committed by *Endeavour*, and that is why they did not allow the protest. The theory was a boat that had already committed a foul could not disqualify another boat.

The fifth race was exciting because halfway out on the first half of the race, the boatswain of *Rainbow* was knocked overboard by a sudden intentional gybe. He hung onto the end of the backstay, although he was being pulled along under water and was finally pulled aboard. Had he let go, the *Rainbow* would have had to stop and pick him up and would have lost the race. As it was, *Rainbow* went on to win decisively, by 4 minutes.

In the sixth race, there was much maneuvering at the start, and before they were across the line both boats were flying protest flags. *Endeavour* was ahead to begin with, but by superior sailing and sail handling the *Rainbow* crew managed to come up, pass her, and win the race by 55 seconds. Both protests were withdrawn that night, but it could not be said that the races of 1934 ended in international amity.

Three years later, Sopwith came back again to race in J-boats, with *Endeavour II,* a boat that was even faster than the first *Endeavour.* Since it was generally acknowledged that the British boat of 1934 was by far better than *Rainbow,* and that the American victory had been due almost entirely to Vanderbilt's sailing ability and his selection of men, it was apparent to the Americans that they would have to build a new defender for 1937.

This year the full effect of the shortage of money in America was felt in the matter of defense of The Cup. No syndicate could be formed to build the new J-boat, and eventually Harold Vanderbilt put up the money alone, bearing what might have seemed to him the dubious honor of being first individual owner of a Cup defender since General Paine, who defended with *Volunteer* in 1887.

No figures were released concerning the cost of *Ranger,* but even by using all that was salvageable from *Rainbow* the cost was estimated to be more than $150,000, and before The Cup races were held the cost of preparing for the defense was placed at around a half million dollars.

From England, while it was indicated that *Endeavour II* would be the challenger, Sopwith was not quite certain until he had tested his second boat against the first, and so the challenger was not actually named in the challenge. Sopwith, who had the right to name the date of the first race, studied his North American weather reports and picked July 31.

Ranger was launched at the Bath Iron Works in Maine on July 11, and three days later Harold Vanderbilt's steam yacht *Vara* began towing her down the Kennebec River, on her way to finishing and racing. The yacht moved outside the estuary with its tow and all seemed to be well as night fell. At about midnight, the crew heard a clanging noise aloft, and discovered that one of the upper rigging spans, between the second and third spreaders, had been carried away, leaving the last 70 feet of the 165 foot mast unsupported.

The mast began to sway. The two vessels were traveling in a quartering swell, which made the swaying regular and fairly heavy. With each

Endeavour II

Ranger

movement the rigging went slack and then went taut, and the whole rig began to come loose. By dawn more stays had broken away and the top 130 feet of the mast was unsupported and whipping back and forth like a rapier. Finally, the twisting had its effect and the mast snapped off just above the lower spreaders to go over the side and hang down, endangering the hull. The crew freed the wreckage and dropped the mast into 60 fathoms of water. So instead of a proud racer, *Vara* towed a dismasted hulk into Marblehead the next day.

It was just a few days before the races were to begin and Vanderbilt needed a mast. The Bath Iron Works was put to work to duplicate *Ranger's* original mast, and for the meantime *Rainbow's* mast was made to do.

The hull of *Rainbow* was purchased by Chandler Hovey and refitted to make a new try for The Cup defense. *Yankee* had been changed somewhat, and she was was to try also.

This year there were two sets of trials, one set for defender and one set for challenger, with Sopwith bringing both his boats to see which would be faster in American waters.

There was really no question after the first few races as to which boat would be named defender. With a jury rig, *Ranger* still defeated the others in races and by convincing margins of 5 minutes and more. In one of the trials, too, Harold Vanderbilt showed his mastery of the sailing craft by setting a huge spinnaker of 18,000 square feet, the largest sail ever set on a yacht, and then gybing with it set. He managed this by setting another spinnaker boom on the same side of the mainsail and forward of the sail. Later the committee held this to be illegal.

The races began on the named date of July 31, in an atmosphere of some mystery. Sopwith had never let the Americans see which of his boats was fastest because he maneuvered them constantly but did not race. (He knew he was going to use *Endeavour II* and so *Endeavour I* was partly used to confuse the opponents.) Then *Endeavour I* sailed in two informal races just before The Cup contests. In the first race she finished dead last, with *Ranger* winning. In the second *Endeavour I* finished first with *Ranger* in third place. This still said nothing about *Endeavour II.*

On the day of the first race, the contest was delayed because 800 excursion steamers, small yachts, and even tiny catboats had crowded into the area around Brenton Reef lightship to see what they could of the contest.

Finally the race began. Vanderbilt broke out an enormous Genoa jib very quickly and got it up where it pulled steadily. This time, Sopwith had a professional crew instead of the amateurs he had brought in 1934, but the professionals still could not hold the *Ranger,* and she won by 17 minutes.

In the second race *Ranger* won by an even greater margin—18 minutes and 32 seconds. In the third race, even though *Ranger* ran into trouble when a winch jammed, she still won by more than 4 minutes. By the time the fourth race was to be sailed the challengers knew they could not beat the American boat except on a fluke, and they were relaxed. They sailed a good race, outsailing *Ranger* on one reach, but the defender still won by a margin of well over 3 minutes, and that was the end of the series, a series won by the fastest J-boat ever built anywhere.

13

The Twelve-Meters

The races of 1937 were the last to be held for The America's Cup for 20 years, and the reason, of course, was the coming of World War II and the serious economic problems that beset the world for the first dozen years after the war.

By the 1950's there was no possibility that the J-boats would ever race again. They were too big and too expensive to build, to maintain, or to race. It would have cost a half a million dollars to build such a boat, and a million dollars to make a defense. Indeed, as early as 1930 one American syndicate had spent $900,000 in trying to put its defender into the races. A quarter of a century later the cost would have been double.

The only way The America's Cup races could be continued would be to go to a much smaller class of boats, and this was discussed from time to time among yachtsmen in the United States and England.

Eventually the yachtsmen settled on a class called the Twelve-Meter Class International Rule Sloops, which might be about 70 feet overall with a 45 foot waterline. Next to a J-boat they would be regarded as dwarfs, yet they were seaworthy and fast boats in their own right as a class.

In June, 1957, the Royal Yacht Squadron challenged again, for races to be held in September of 1958, four of seven to decide the winner of the Cup.

The British boat was called *Sceptre,* and she was of a design underwater that had not been seen in the United States for a long time. Cod's head and mackerel's tail, they called it, meaning that she had heavy, full forward sections and fine slim after parts.

One of the American boats which hoped to defend this year was *Vim,* owned by Captain John N. Mathews and sailed by his sons as captain and navigator. Later she was commanded by the well—known racing captain Emil "Bus" Mosbacher.

Another American boat was *Columbia,* built for a syndicate led by Henry Sears and Briggs Cunningham, and sailed under Cunningham, who had considerable experience in 12-meter boats before the war.

Two other boats, *Weatherly* and *Easterner,* hoped to compete, but did not manage to work themselves up in time to give much showing in the preliminary races.

In the New York Yacht Club's annual outing, *Vim* showed herself to be the top boat, and it seemed likely that she would be the defender that year. She won five of the seven races, *Columbia* winning the other two.

Still, the decision would be made after the official trials. There was a change in racing procedure for 12 meters. The windward-and-return course consisted of two roundings of a 6 mile course—24 miles in all. The triangular course consisted of three legs of 8 miles each in all. A special America's Cup buoy was set out 9 miles south-southeast of Brenton Reef lightship, because the J-boats, with long courses to sail, had earlier needed to start to leeward when the wind was offshore and this system gave sea room for starting all races to windward.

In the official trials the four American boats raced for three days, then *Weatherly* and *Easterner* were eliminated, and it was between *Vim* and *Columbia.*

In the first match *Columbia* beat *Vim* easily in heavy wind. In the second *Vim* won by 10 seconds, through superior handling. *Columbia* won the third race. *Vim* won the fourth by outmaneuvering *Columbia* again. In the fifth race on the windward-leeward course *Columbia* won again, and then came a sixth race, which was so closely contested that at the second turn *Columbia* led by 9 seconds, and eventually won the race by 12 seconds.

Columbia then, was declared the defender.

Captain of the challenging *Sceptre* was Lt. Commander Graham Mann, an Olympic racing champion, though not in 12-meter boats. Briggs Cunningham was captain of the *Columbia* and Henry Sears was navigator. Oddly enough, in each yacht there was a member of the Ratsey family, sailmakers for a century, who had long been active in America's Cup affairs.

These were small vessels compared to the old ones. *Columbia* was 45 feet, 9 inches long at the waterline and *Sceptre* was 46 feet, 6 inches long. Both carried about 1,950 square feet of sail—a far cry from the 16,000 feet of the old sailing scows.

This time a thousand small boats lined up to watch the race, and some not so small. President Eisenhower was there aboard the *USS Mitscher.* The public was ready for a great battle.

But there was no battle. *Sceptre's* design had failed her—so much was obvious from the start to the experts. Cunningham got the better start in

Sceptre

Weatherly

Columbia, but *Sceptre* never did get properly started, it seemed. In 5 minutes *Columbia* had a 7 length lead. By the halfway mark it seemed apparent that *Columbia* had won. Win she did, although the boats nearly lost their wind and the race. The breeze finally picked up enough so that the boats could get going, and *Sceptre* picked up enough in sailing so that she cut the lead of *Columbia* to 7 minutes and 94 seconds. But in 12 meters, that was scarcely much of a race.

Yachtsmen could see that *Sceptre* was no match for *Columbia* in light breezes. The British backers talked then about how well *Sceptre* performed in heavy weather, and everyone was hoping for a "sou'wester" of 25 knots or so for the next race.

Instead, there was no wind at all. The race was begun in light breezes, and ended in no breeze at all, with *Columbia* ahead, but 4 miles from the finish line.

On September 24 the next race was held, in a wind that varied between 8 and 12 knots, but *Sceptre* was most disappointing. She did not seem to handle any better than she had in light breezes, and *Columbia* won by 11 minutes and 42 seconds.

In the third race there really was a breeze. The wind was blowing at 22 miles an hour at the start and harder later. But an hour after the start *Columbia* led by 2 minutes and 23 seconds, and when they turned and roared downwind at 10 knots under big spinnakers, *Sceptre* did not gain. Then turning again and sailing into the wind, *Sceptre* lost more ground and finished up 8 minutes and 20 seconds behind.

The last race was held the next day. *Sceptre* overshot the mark at the start and had to go back, giving *Columbia* a lead. *Columbia* stayed between *Sceptre* and the mark all the way, giving her as much blanket as she could on some 8 tacks, and rounding the mark 5½ minutes ahead. Then *Sceptre's* jibsheet fouled a cleat and had to be cut loose. Her spinnaker guy parted and the end broke off the pole, and then she broke her main boom. She sailed the race out, however, with her crew repairing the boom while under way, and although she lost by several minutes, it was remarkable that she finished at all. So the seventeenth challenge for The America's Cup was defeated.

The next challenge for the Cup was made in 1962, and this time it came from Australia, for the first time in the history of The America's Cup. A syndicate was formed to make the challenge by Sir Frank Packer. The old America's Cup hopeful *Vim* was purchased and taken to Australia to give designers an eye for the 12-meter class and also to give the challenger, which was to be named *Gretel,* something to work out against which would approximate the American defender. *Gretel* was launched in the spring and began her trials in home waters in April.

Meanwhile in the United States several groups hoped to win the right to defend The Cup. F.E. Hood designed a boat in Boston which was backed by a Boston syndicate. Before the summer was well along there were four contenders, *Nefertiti, Columbia, Easterner,* and *Weatherly,* which was captained by Bus Mosbacher. *Columbia* and *Easterner* were eliminated rather quickly in the trial races. *Nefertiti* was a contender all the way. She was damaged one night when her mooring lines were cut, but not too seriously and she came back to sail strongly against *Weatherly* in the trials. *Weatherly,* however, won races on August 24, 25, and 26, and was then named to be the American defender for 1962.

Gretel and *Vim* were brought to the United States for final conditioning, and there *Gretel's* mast was moved forward a few feet in the hope that this would give her additional speed in the American waters.

Newport was busy that fall. Every hotel room was booked. Each crew had its own house, rented for several thousand dollars for the short season, and all the houses at Newport were in use, it seemed. Given the impetus of The America's Cup races, the old millionaires' playground was coming back into the public eye.

The first race of 1962 was scheduled for September 16, and both crews spent the last two days working up to it. This year the defender's crew was one hundred percent amateur. Captain Mosbacher was a real estate investor; others included a lithography salesman, an insurance broker, a photo studio operator, a whiskey salesman, a glass fibre salesman, a shipping executive, two owners of a stevedoring firm, and two college students. They lived in one of the Newport "cottages" and worked every day on *Weatherly.*

Gretel seemed dogged by hard luck, before the race began. She broke her boom on September 12. Then two days later, when she was hauled for a look at her hull, she slipped off the support blocks, and there was considerable fear that her hull had been damaged. Fortunately it had not, and she was ready on September 16, when the boats moved out to the markers near the reef.

The first race was sailed in a 15 knot breeze, which definitely favored *Weatherly,* since she was known to respond quickly in light airs. She won, without difficulty, by 3 minutes and 46 seconds, on a windward-leeward course.

The second race was sailed in weather much more to *Gretel's* liking, over the triangular course. The breeze turned into a 25 knot northwest wind that day, with heavy swells and whitecaps. *Gretel's* crew was very pleased. At the start, Mosbacher managed to gain a 5 length lead, but then in order

Columbia

Gretel

to protect it, he had to tack every time the following boat tacked, in order to blanket her and keep her from coming up on him. Australian skipper Jock Sturrock tacked 11 times in 5 minutes, trying to wear out the crew of *Weatherly*. He seemed not only to make up part of the difference in the tacking, but to tire the crew of the American defender, for at the first buoy *Weatherly's* lead was cut to only 12 seconds or 2 boat lengths.

The racers turned around the mark and then headed for the next buoy, 8 miles away. By the time they reached this marker, *Weatherly* was still ahead, now by 14 seconds, but then *Gretel* put up her big spinnaker and began to gain on *Weatherly*. When *Weatherly's* spinnaker pole snapped under the strain of the brisk breeze, it was all up with the defender, so close was the race. *Gretel* passed her and came home winner by 47 seconds, having sailed the fastest America's Cup race ever sailed in 12-meter boats. The time was 2 hours, 46 minutes and 47 seconds for the course of a little more than 24 miles.

That night in Newport the Australians celebrated, for they had won the first victory gained by a challenger for The Cup in 14 races that ran back to 1934. *Weatherly* was still favored for the series of 4-out-of-7, but the Australians now had their hopes up.

But that was the end of the heavy weather. The third race was sailed in very light breezes that reached a 10 knot maximum, and *Weatherly* won by 8 minutes and 40 seconds. The fourth race was more exciting. Captain Sturrock was behind by 1½ minutes at the first of the three buoys around the triangle, but he pulled up until on the last leg it seemed that he might catch *Weatherly,* and had the course been longer this could have happened. As it was, *Weatherly* won by a single length.

Then came the fifth race, sailed on September 26, and the Americans won again, handily, to take the series and keep The Cup, as everyone then expected.

In the autumn of 1962 the British Royal Thames Yacht Club issued a challenge for 1963, which was refused by the New York Yacht Club. Defense of The America's Cup, even with the coming of the 12-meter boats, was growing so expensive that it could not be undertaken every year.

The 12-meters, which had replaced the expensive J-boats, were now almost prohibitively expensive to build and maintain. In 1964 a 12-meter defender could cost a quarter of a million dollars.

The New York Yacht Club declined to defend in 1963 and precipitated a brief, bitter argument. The British club responded that if the New York Yacht Club would not defend, then The Cup belonged to the British by default. The argument was settled, however, when the Americans agreed to defend in 1964 and the British agreed to the conditions of challenge, which were generally those of the past.

In 1963 however, the British did not name their challenger immediately. Two British boats were in competition for the right to race, the *Kurrewa,* which was favored to win, and the *Sovereign.* Several syndicates were formed in the United States, including one by P. S. du Pont, which said it would spend as much as $475,000 for its boat. *Columbia,* now owned by T. P. Dougan, was again a contender for the honor of defending. *Easterner* and *Nefertiti* were also in the running, and when it was launched, the Du Pont syndicate's boat, *American Eagle,* was a prime contender. There was one other, *Constellation,* built by a competing syndicate.

The races were scheduled to begin September 16. The trials continued through August, for both sides. The British finally chose *Sovereign,* which had proved far more successful in American waters than *Kurrewa.* *Columbia* and *Nefertiti* were eliminated from the American competition on August 21, and then, early in September, *Constellation* was named over *American Eagle* after defeating her in the trials decisively.

Peter Scott, son of Polar Explorer Robert F. Scott, was the skipper of the *Sovereign.* Eric Ridder and Robert N. Bavier, Jr., were co-captains and helmsmen of the *Constellation.* They were all good sailing men.

The boats were a different matter. Money seemed to count, for *Constellation,* which had cost $700,000 to build and equip, was so far superior to *Sovereign,* which had cost $300,000, that there was no question in anyone's mind as to the victor in the series, unless it was in the hopes of the British sailors.

The races began on September 16 over the two courses. In the first race, *Constellation* won by 5 minutes, 34 seconds, a very long time in 12-meter racing.

The second race was sailed two days after the first, on September 18. The wind was good and fresh at 20 knots, and it was said that this was just what *Sovereign* wanted. All week the British had been talking about the need for strong breezes if their hopes were to hold up. At the start, *Sovereign* moved into the lead by 5 lengths, but thereafter *Constellation* came up on her, passed her and went away so rapidly that the race finished with *Constellation* 20 minutes and 24 seconds ahead, the largest margin of victory ever won in a 12-meter cup race.

Constellation won the the third race handily over the triangular course, by 6 minutes and 33 seconds, and then, on September 22, as expected, she won the final race and The Cup was secure for the nineteenth time since the *America* won it away from the Royal Yacht Squadron's summer

Constellation

Sovereign

fleet so long before.

That same autumn, an Australian syndicate challenged again, setting the date as 1967 for the races, and it was announced, even before the tank testing had begun or designs or work had been thought through for the new Australian challenger, that the yacht would cost at least $380,000.

Once again, as with the J-boats, cup racing was growing so expensive that the conservatives among the yachtsmen were talking about necessary changes in the system.

One thing was certain, however, in the expensive years of the 1960's: as long as there was an America's Cup there would be challengers and defenders, even if they finally decided to race in dinghies.

14

Enter the *Dame Pattie*

Two years after the defeat of *Sovereign*, the Australians were again ready to challenge the New York Yacht Club defender for The America's Cup and after all the usual negotiations it was agreed that the Australian 12-meter yacht *Dame Pattie* come to the east coast of North America.

The *Dame Pattie* was very much a community enterprise "down under." She was backed by a syndicate of 15 major companies, representing everything from cigarettes to sail cloth. As had become the pattern in the United States, the honor of defending for The Cup holders was hotly contested, this year between four yachts, the old *Constellation* of the previous defense, and yachts named *American Eagle, Columbia,* and *Intrepid.* The last was the new entry of the usual New York Yacht Club syndicate—or one of them—and Emil "Bus" Mosbacher Jr., was again chosen skipper of this particular boat, designed by Olin Stephens.

All spring and summer yachting circles were abuzz with arguments about the qualities of the various boats, but finally the New York Club picked *Intrepid* after she had outclassed all comers in the usual trials. The matter of selection was becoming more and more technical, more hairlines were being considered than ever before. Still there were three important factors in yacht racing, as always: the hull, the sails, and the crew. But to show how complex matters had become, in 1967's challenge, the *Intrepid* syndicate spent $40,000 in 18 months, with naval architect Stephens testing 8 different hull models and 35 modifications before he arrived at the final design of *Intrepid's* hull.

By the time that *Dame Pattie* arrived in eastern waters, all the details were well along. The yachts would race, as in 1964, over a course consisting of six legs, instead of the old windward-leeward and triangular layouts. Four of the six legs would be sailed on the long side (4.5 miles) of a triangle and three would be to windward. The other sides would be broad reaches—assuming, which one could do only hopefully, that the wind did not change during the course of a race. This year there would be
96

33 Navy and Coast Guard vessels patrolling to prevent interference of spectators with the course of the races.

As far as their performances in respective home waters were concerned, it was apparent that *Dame Pattie* and *Intrepid* were the best representatives of their countries. In 13 trials against the old *Gretel,* the Australians' previous contender, *Dame Pattie* had won 11 races. *Intrepid's* success story was even more spectacular; in 19 trials against the other three American yachts, *Intrepid* had won 18 times, losing only to *American Eagle,* and that in the second preliminary trial off Stamford on June 6.

Early in September the crews and supporters began to gather in Newport, where, as usual, the hotels were filled to overflowing and latecomers were reduced to taking what they could find in rooming houses. Eleven excursions steamers were laid on in various nearby ports, and hundreds of yachtsmen planned to come and drop anchor in Newport Harbor. They would have to anchor, for every available mooring space in the dock area had long been reserved.

Soon it was announced that the first race would be held on September 12, weather permitting. Jock Sturrock would again skipper the Australian challenger, it was said. As usual, on the evening of September 11, newspapermen were bedevilling all the skippers and designers and syndicate members for predictions as to the outcome. Chairman Henry S. Morgan of the race committee was overwhelmed with last minute details as usual, and the tension increased hour by hour.

The Australians were very confident, but privately so, and would not be drawn into predictions. Australian designer Warwick Hood said the only way he would make a prediction is if he knew what had come out of the *Intrepid's* tank tests—and he did not. As for *Dame Pattie,* he said, he had set out to build a boat that would respond at her best in light, variable breezes, with winds under 15 knots. He had done so, and he was satisfied. Further, he said hopefully, she had turned out to be a fine performer in heavy weather, and although she had been dismasted in one of the trials—which accounted for the first defeat by *Gretel*—all was well with her.

Skipper Sturrock would not venture an opinion. Neither would American designer Stephens, and all American skipper Mosbacher would say was that the Americans had a healthy respect for *Dame Pattie* and the Australian crew and were very much on edge.

The newspapermen then were reduced to speculating among themselves as to the outcome, and they joined a thousand yachtsmen in that pastime. The records of the past were brought out and examined over again. Many experts said they thought the previous meeting between Sturrock and Mosbacher had proved the Australians to have a better boat in *Gretel* in 1962, and the Americans to have the more capable skipper in Mosbacher—and that was what had accounted for the four American victories to one Australian victory.

As the yachts were made ready, the flags of the New York Yacht Club flew high along with those of the Royal Sydney Yacht Squadron. On September 11, day before the first race was scheduled, 30-knot winds northeasterly came up to remind all concerned that September was hurricane season along the eastern American coast. Actually, far to the south Hurricane Doria was kicking up huge seas and foul winds for fair, but at Newport the 30-knot wind and choppy seas were simply reminders, and Committee Chairman Morgan said he was not so much worried about the ability of the yachts to race as the problem of securing the Navy tugs that would be used as rounding marks for the races. There could be no race if the tugs could not be anchored safely, he said.

By late afternoon on September 11, the wind was dropping and was expected to blow at about 10-20 knots from the northeast the following morning. *Dame Pattie* was given a new backstay that day, and then the two yachts and their captains went about the formal business of readying for the race. They met wtih representatives of the committee and agreed to abide by the rules of the race, then received their sailing instructions. Both yachts were tested for flotation, which meant checked to be sure that they lived up to a very complex formula.*

$$* \ \text{Rating} = \underline{\frac{L + 2d + \sqrt{SA} \text{-} F}{2.37}} \quad = 12 \text{ Meters} = R$$

$$L = Li + 1\tfrac{1}{2} (Gf\text{-}2x.05R) + 1/3 (Ga\text{-}2a)$$

$$d = 2 (ACB\text{-}AB)$$

SA=Sail area. F=Average freeboard, from measurements taken at three different places. R=Rating to International 12-Meter rule. Li=Imaginary waterline 1.5% of R above designed waterline. Gf=Girth forward. Ga=Girth aft. ACB=skin-girth measurement amidships. AB=Chain-girth measurement amidships.

The idea of these limits was still to give designers a certain amount of leeway in planning a yacht, yet make it possible for them to race as equal competitors. Extreme changes in one area such as length had to be paid for by alterations in another area such as sail. Theoretically a 12-meter could be the size of a canoe with huge sail area (except that it would capsize under the sail), or it could have a clipper ship hull and a sailing

Dame Pattie

Intrepid

dinghy sail (except that it would not move except in a hurricane). Over the years the 12-meter class had developed into a general standard of 65 feet long with sail areas around 2000 square feet. But the minor variations were very important and contributed much to the winning or losing of races. Designer Stephens had used the tank tests to show him that he wanted a shortened keel, which he produced, and a "kicker" or skeg aft, plus changing the lines to copy those of an Indian canoe. By doing all this he had reduced the eddies in the wake that tugged at the stern of the yacht and kept speed down. Now on the day before the race, the spectators began comparing the yachts.

COMPARISON

	Dame Pattie	Intrepid
Overall Length	64 feet	65 feet 2 inches
Waterline	45 feet 6 inches	46 feet 11 inches
Beam	12 feet	11 feet 11 inches
Draft	9 feet	9 feet 1 inch
Sail Area	1850 square feet	1795 square feet
Displacement	57,000 pounds	58,000 pounds

They were ready on the morning of September 12. Course signals would be given at 11:50, a warning signal would come at noon, a preparatory signal at 12:05, and they would be away at 12:10. *Intrepid* with her white hull would wear Sail Number U.S. 22, and *Dame Pattie* with ice-blue hull would wear Sail Number KA 2. The odds quoted in the local smoke shops were 4 to 1 in favor of the American defender.

At the starting gun the air was cool with unlimited visibility and a bright sun; the wind was 18 knots and the sea, with white caps flaking off the tops of the waves, was running 3 feet.

At the start the Americans had the best of it. Mosbacher planted *Intrepid* on the weather beam of the Australian challenger, and having secured that advantage at the beginning, boat and crew outsailed their rivals all the way. After 12 minutes it was apparent that barring an accident the *Intrepid* would win. At the end of the first leg (4.5 miles) *Intrepid* was ahead by 1 minute, 50 seconds, she gained 21 seconds and 39 seconds on the next two legs, or spinnaker reaches, picked up another minute and 36 seconds on the next windward leg, and that is how it went—on every leg she moved out a bit further ahead. It was only for that first dozen minutes that it appeared to be a race, and then the Australian lack of experience showed. On the first tack Skipper Sturrock came about under *Intrepid's* stern to gain the wind, but on his second tack his crew misjudged, the *Dame Pattie* was rolled by a wave, the crew fumbled the trimming of the jib sheet and the yacht fell off to leeward, losing time. On the first setting of her spinnaker, when replacing a Genoa jib, the Genoa was dragged over the side, which did not help, and then in jibbing at turn to begin the second reach leg, the spinnaker let go the pole at the clew and became a hindrance instead of a help. It was 4 minutes before the sail was recovered.

At the end, and in the inevitable postmortem conducted by the press, the Aussies admitted that the wind had been a little more than they had expected for Newport. Australian sailing water is strong weather water, but in thier previous trip to Newport the Australians felt they had been beaten largely because their boat was designed for heavy weather and the breezes were light, so they had designed a light-breeze boat. They said she should go well also in heavier weather, but she did not seem to.

The second race was sailed the next day. The wind was much more to *Dame Pattie's* liking, and she sailed much better, and for the first few minutes of the race she was ahead. *Intrepid* sailed through her lee, crossed on tack two lengths ahead of the Australian challenger and began a battle of short tacks. At the end of 6 tacks, the *Dame Pattie* had made up a length of the distance. Then the crew flubbed the handling of the jib, fouling it while trimming the sheet going from the port to starboard tack. The yacht was caught in stays and stood shivering in the wind for several seconds. By the time she dropped back to the port tack she had lost 3 boat lengths. Even so it was still a race as far as the first Navy tug that marked the end of the opening leg and the beginning of a spinnaker reach. But on both the spinnaker reaches *Dame Pattie* lost heavily.

Some time was regained, yet on the next to last leg it was apparent to Sturrock that he could not win unless he did something desperate, so he gybed high of the course, while Mosbacher sailed true. Skipper Sturrock made a broad reach on this run to enjoy a faster sailing angle. But he did not catch the different breeze he sought, and wound up sailing further in the same wind, and losing more time.

By this time the consensus at Newport was that *Dame Pattie* was neither the yacht nor her crew the crew to beat Mosbacher and his men in The Cup series. The third race was sailed the next day, and the defender was ahead from the beginning and won by 4 minutes and 41 seconds, with *Dame Pattie* three quarters of a mile in her wake. The most exciting incident of the day occurred when a Coast Guard helicopter came in so close over a 12-foot catboat that its downdraft capsized the boat, and the helicopter then had to rescue the crew. That same draft affected the

Intrepid, too, for the helicopter had come in to shoo the catboat off the course, and Skipper Mosbacher noticed the blast of the rotors. Still, he needed no excuses. One other point was clear: the Australians were suffering from a bad guess about the Newport weather, for *Dame Pattie* was a breeze boat, not a weather boat, and she showed it this day, burying her lee rail deep in the swells under a Genoa jib, and hobbyhorsing to fling white water out noticeably, while *Intrepid* stood up straight and sped along. In this race the Australian crew sailed better, with but one fumble, however as usual, the highly trained, skilled American crew did not make a single mistake. Even when the helicopter swooped down on them to drive off the catboat, and Mosbacher had to bear off so sharply that the yacht's mainsail wrapped around the backstay, the yacht slipped alee a hundred yards, and lost perhaps 30 seconds in time—the incident was handled coolly and did not affect the outcome.

There was no race on Friday. *Dame Pattie's* skipper asked for a day off, and there would have been no race in any event, because the wind blew up to gale force. Hurricane Doria was at it again.

Saturday and Sunday the weather was better, except that on Sunday as the race was about to begin, the fog set in across the course and the meeting had to be called off. The Australians expected little, for they knew they had neither boat nor crew to win this year. They were proved right when *Intrepid* walked off with the last race too, to take the series in four straight and retain the cup once again.

Once again there was talk of retiring The Cup or of changing the contest to a one-design contest, which would eliminate the matter of naval architecture from The America's Cup challenges and make the victory a matter of crews and skippers. But the majority of those in control believed that to do so would be to change the whole concept: there was no question of one design when the *America* walked off with the cup in the beginning, she raced against all comers and her design was a vital factor in her victory. Also, in 1967 there was no shortage of challengers, even though 12-meter yacht building and racing was growing ever more expensive. A French team was ready to challenge for 1970. So were two or three English teams. The end of The America's Cup was not yet in sight, nor was the end of 12-meter racing.

Bibliography

Coffin, Roland R. *The America's Cup.* New York: Charles Scribner's Sons, 1885.

Kemp, P. K. *Racing for the America's Cup.* London: Hutchinson and Company, 1937.

Lindsay, Nigel. *The America's Cup.* London: Heath Crane Ltd., 1930.

Stone, H. L. and Taylor, W. H., *The America's Cup Races.* Princeton, New Jersey: D. Van Nostrand Company, 1958.

Also the files of *Yachting, The New York Times, Time Magazine* and *Sports Illustrated* were consulted in the preparation of this book.

Index

105